CANADA'S UNITY CRISIS

Implications for ☆ U.S.–Canadian ⚜ Economic Relations

by Earl H. Fry

A Twentieth Century Fund Paper

The Twentieth Century Fund Press/New York/ 1992

The Twentieth Century Fund is a research foundation undertaking timely analyses of economic, political, and social issues. Not-for-profit and non-partisan, the Fund was founded in 1919 and endowed by Edward A. Filene.

Library of Congress Cataloging-in-Publication Data

Fry, Earl H.
    Canada's unity crisis: implications for U.S.-Canadian economic relations / by Earl H. Fry.
        p.   cm.
    "A Twentieth Century Fund paper."
    Includes bibliographical references and index.
    ISBN 0-87078-335-1 : $8.95
    1. Canada—Foreign economic relations—United States. 2. United States—Foreign economic relations—Canada. 3. Canada—Politics and government—1980- 4. Québec (Province)—Politics and government—1960- 5. Political culture—Canada. I. Title.
HF1480.15.U5F79 1992
337.71073—dc20

92-32165
CIP

Cover Design and Illustration: Claude Goodwin
Manufactured in the United States of America.
Copyright © 1992 by the Twentieth Century Fund, Inc.

Canada's Unity Crisis

FOREWORD

On October 26, 1992, Canadians will determine the future of their nation. The national referendum that is being held on that day marks the culmination of a crisis of unity that has plagued the country on and off for more than a decade. The crisis—perhaps the most profound in Canada's history—is the result of past failures to resolve the question of Quebec's role in the Canadian confederation. Whatever the outcome of the current constitutional debate, the changes set in motion have important implications not only for the Canadian economy and political system, but also for its closest neighbor and largest trading partner, the United States.

This referendum is taking place in the midst of—and might have serious consequences for—a critical phase of the debate about the recently negotiated North American Free Trade Agreement (NAFTA), an agreement that would create a partial economic union among the United States, Canada, and Mexico. The world's seventh-largest economy, Canada is the United States' largest trading partner, with over $200 billion in goods and services crossing the border annually. Almost one-quarter of all U.S. merchandise exports are destined for Canada. In contrast, the United States exports less than 10 percent of its goods to Mexico. Yet the impact of reduced trade barriers with Mexico, not Canada, is the focus of much of the debate in the United States over NAFTA. This focus reflects the much wider economic and cultural differences between the United States and Mexico, and it results from the prior existence of the U.S.-Canada Free Trade Agreement of 1989; but it may also reveal that U.S. citizens take for granted their neighbor to the north.

Earl H. Fry's monograph for the Twentieth Century Fund helps redress this imbalance in attention. Fry, professor of political science at Brigham Young University, succinctly presents the long and complex journey that brought Canada to this moment of decision. For many in the United States, it is difficult to comprehend how a country as seemingly stable and secure as Canada came to face so serious a threat to its future.

The role of the Twentieth Century Fund is to explore current international and national economic and public policy issues. We are pleased that Fry's study builds on two earlier Fund papers on Canada: Gilbert Winham's *Trading with Canada: The Canada-U.S. Free Trade Agreement* and Joel Sokolsky's *Defending Canada: U.S.-Canadian Defense Policies.* It also complements current projects examining new issues in the Western hemisphere involving trade and economic relations, the role of national and international institutions, and U.S. foreign policy in the region.

Although aware that the United States is simply a bystander in the resolution of Canada's constitutional crisis, Fry shows why decisionmakers in the executive branch, on Capitol Hill, and in corporate headquarters throughout the United States have a vested interest in the fate of Canada: the resolution of Canada's unity crisis will affect both our economic future and the future of the hemisphere.

Richard C. Leone, *President*
The Twentieth Century Fund
September 1992

CONTENTS

CHAPTER ONE

CANADA'S STRATEGIC AND ECONOMIC IMPORTANCE TO THE UNITED STATES

C anada celebrated a bittersweet 125th anniversary as a nation in 1992, bittersweet because many Canadians fear that their country may soon fall apart. And the danger is self-imposed. In 1991, the Quebec government passed a law requiring that a referendum be held before the end of October 1992 to decide whether the people of Quebec want to remain within Canada. If Quebec voters opt for sovereignty or reject a new constitutional package offered by the rest of the nation, Canada may go the way of the former Soviet Union, Yugoslavia, and Czechoslovakia, although separation will be more in the spirit of the "velvet divorce" of the Czechs and the Slovaks than the rampant violence that accompanied the breakup of the Yugoslavian republics.

Over the past several months, representatives of federal, provincial, and territorial governments and aboriginal groups have met to consider major revisions in Canada's constitution. These delegates have now recommended major constitutional changes in the parliamentary structure, the selection of Supreme Court judges, the division of powers between Ottawa and the provincial governments, and the status of Quebec within confederation. They also support the inherent right of aboriginals

26 Th

to self-government and the opportunity for aboriginal groups to form the third official level of government within Canada's federal system. All of these monumental changes are being contemplated during Canada's struggle to emerge from its worst economic downturn since the Great Depression. With little doubt, the challenges facing Canada in the 1990s are the greatest it has faced in peacetime during the twentieth century; they will determine the viability of Canadian nationhood and dramatically affect Canada's ability to compete in the global economy.

Canada's Strategic Importance

For many years, Americans have considered the Canadians and the British as their best friends in the world, but they actually know very little of substance about Canada. One American reporter has referred to Canada as "the biggest invisible land mass in the world."[1] Television's fictional reporter Murphy Brown has provided her own acerbic view of the typical Canadian evening news summary: "Moose loose, moose caught, more snow, good night!"[2] Even President Dwight Eisenhower once introduced John Diefenbaker as the Prime Minister of that "Great Republic of Canada," ignoring that Canada is a constitutional monarchy.[3] Canadians often complain that the American awareness of Canada rarely goes beyond the "3-M" stereotyped image of moose, mountains, and Mounties, and a recent Gallup poll seems to bear this out. When asked to identify the leading trading partner of the United States, 49 percent of Americans selected Japan and only 8 percent correctly named Canada. Furthermore, only 16 percent could identify Canada's capital city and 13 percent the current prime minister of Canada.[4]

Strategically, Canada has always played a vitally important role in U.S. security. Both nations were founding members of the North Atlantic Treaty Organization (NATO) in 1949 and of the North American Aerospace Defense Command (NORAD) in 1957. Canada is also the one nation on earth that, from a polar vantage point, physically separates the United States' and Russian military superpowers. And Americans and Canadians fought together in World War I, World War II, the Korean War, and the Persian Gulf War.

Until recently, the creation of an independent Quebec nation on the northern border of the United States would have introduced an element of uncertainty unknown in North American relations since Canada became a confederation in 1867. In 1992, the strategic implications of a Quebec referendum are, however, far different from those that were present in May 1980 when Quebec held its last referendum on sovereignty. Back then, the cold war was still frigid and the United States was preparing to boycott the 1980 Summer Olympics in Moscow in retaliation for the Soviet incursion into Afghanistan. Moreover, Americans greatly feared both the spread of communism and socialism in the Western Hemisphere. Thus, even though the popularly elected Parti Québécois (PQ) government espoused social-democratic principles similar to those in Scandinavia, some Americans began to refer to Quebec as the "Cuba of the north." Understandably, PQ leaders concentrated on the economic and structural adjustments that would have to be made at home if Quebec were to become an independent country and, consequently, did not pay much attention to what future role an independent Quebec would assume in the Western alliance. As a result, critics in the United States harbored exaggerated fears that an independent Quebec led by the PQ would abandon NATO and NORAD, form a special relationship with the old mother country, France, and perhaps improve relations with the Soviet Union in return for enhanced trade and investment activity.

The world is now far different. The cold war is over, the Soviet Union no longer exists, communism is moribund, and the two major military powers, the United States and Russia, have agreed to pare their strategic nuclear arsenals by two-thirds. Both the Liberal party of Quebec and the PQ are devoted to the defense of the West and to what remains of NATO and NORAD. As a result, the strategic-military implications of an independent Quebec for the United States are presently quite minor, and the North American relationship would continue to be relatively secure with or without a new nation along the 49th parallel.

BILATERAL ECONOMIC LINKAGES

Today and for the foreseeable future, economic ties constitute the most important connection between Canada and the United States. Either the creation of an independent Quebec nation, or radical changes in the structure of the Canadian confederation, could profoundly affect these economic linkages.

It is difficult to overemphasize the critical importance of this bilateral relationship for both the U.S. corporate and labor sectors. The United States and Canada rank, respectively, as the world's largest and seventh largest economies in terms of gross domestic product (GDP). They also enjoy the most expansive bilateral trading relationship in the world, with over $200 billion in goods and services having crossed the 49th parallel in 1991, providing over two million jobs for Canadians and about two million jobs for Americans (see Figure 1).

Almost one-quarter of all U.S. merchandise exports are destined for Canada, slightly less than the amount dispatched annually to the European Community with its twelve member states and 344 million inhabitants. American exports to Canada also surpass the combined U.S. exports to Central and South America, Africa, Western and Eastern Europe (excluding the European Community), Australia, Taiwan, and Hong Kong. From another perspective, the United States exported more in 1990 to one Canadian province, Ontario, than to the nation of Japan; more to Quebec than to Italy; more to British Columbia than to the People's Republic of China; and more to oil-rich Alberta than to the African members of OPEC.

Canada's dependency on access to the vast U.S. marketplace is almost without parallel around the world. In recent years, over 70 percent of all Canadian exports have been destined for the United States, and in recent months, this figure has approached 80 percent. About 30 percent

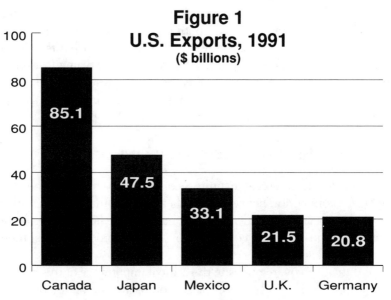

Figure 1
U.S. Exports, 1991
($ billions)

Source: *Survey of Current Business*, March 1992

FDI = foreign direct investment

" 5 of the provinces rely more in intl. trade than on interprovincial trade."

of Canada's income is derived from trade in goods and services (almost twice the level of the United States and three times the level of Japan), and five of the ten provinces actually rely more on international trade than on interprovincial trade. Few citizens of either North American country are aware that U.S. companies and consumers annually purchase one-sixth of everything Canada produces.

Canada is also the leading recipient of U.S. foreign direct investment (FDI) abroad, with U.S. investment north of the border increasing from $49 billion in 1983 to $68 billion at the end of 1991 (see Figure 2). As a proportion of its overall economy, FDI in Canada is much larger than FDI in the United States, and over one-third of Canada's 500 largest industrial firms are foreign-owned, predominantly by Americans. During the mid-1980s, U.S. ownership in Canada accounted for over 70 percent of the assets and over 85 percent of the profits of foreign-owned companies.[5]

In addition to being the leading international direct investor, the United States now ranks as the number one host nation for FDI, with approximately $460 billion (on a historical-cost basis) at the end of 1991. Canada's share of this FDI is $28 billion, providing Canadians with ownership of $228 billion in total U.S. assets, third only to Japan ($370 billion) and

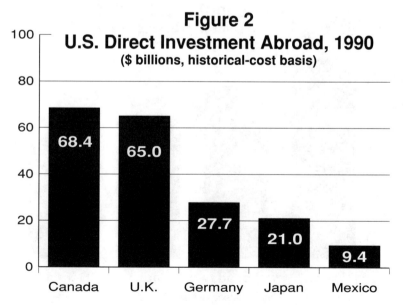

Figure 2
U.S. Direct Investment Abroad, 1990
(\$ billions, historical-cost basis)

Canada	68.4
U.K.	65.0
Germany	27.7
Japan	21.0
Mexico	9.4

Source: *Survey of Current Business*, August 1991

the United Kingdom ($263 billion). Canadian companies also provide 740,000 jobs for American workers, 123,000 more than Japanese firms and 227,000 more than German enterprises (see Figure 3).[6]

International tourism is also at record levels and has been the number one earner of foreign exchange for the United States in each of the past three years, earning more than the export of commercial aircraft, automobiles, chemicals, and agricultural products. Preliminary estimates indicate that over forty million foreign residents visited the United States in 1991 and spent over $50 billion.

Canadians made an astounding seventy-three million border crossings in 1991 (almost three per capita), and in 1992 should account for almost 45 percent of the total number of foreign tourists visiting the United States (see Figure 4). Fifty-nine million of these border crossings in 1991 were one-day trips to buy approximately $5 billion worth of goods in U.S. retail stores.[7] Canadians also prefer to vacation in the United States, and some spend considerable time south of the 49th parallel. For example, the Florida Department of Commerce estimates that five hundred thousand

Figure 3
Employment Provided by Foreign-Owned Firms in the U.S., 1990*
(thousands of U.S. employees)

U.K.: 1,039,200
Canada: 740,000
Japan: 616,700
Germany: 513,300

Source: *Survey of Current Business*, May 1992
*includes employment in all non-bank sectors

Canadians own homes in Florida and another 2.5 million visit each year, indicating that about 10 percent of Canada's entire population may be found in the Sunshine State during the winter months.

Americans made over twelve million trips to Canada in 1991, among the highest number ever recorded.[8] Approximately 90 percent of all international visits to Canada are made by Americans.[9] If the current "Open Skies" negotiations to deregulate airline service between the two countries are successful, this north-south flow of tourists and shoppers may actually increase over the next few years.

> Open Skies negotiations

With over three million jobs tied directly to trade, investment, and tourism linkages with Canada, the United States should be very concerned about what is transpiring north of the border. For far too long, Americans have taken Canada's friendship, stability, and civility for granted. Unfortunately, the Canadian confederation may now be at risk, and the United States' own economic well-being may suffer as a result of the serious problems currently confronting Canada.

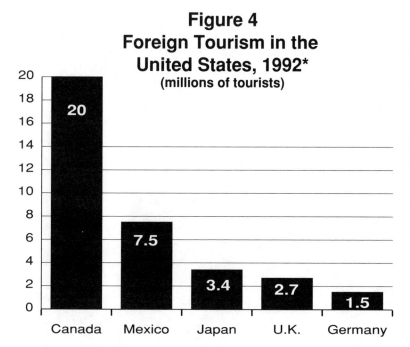

Figure 4
Foreign Tourism in the
United States, 1992*
(millions of tourists)

Source: U.S. Travel and Tourism Administration
*projections for full-year 1992

CHAPTER TWO

UNCERTAINTIES NORTH OF THE 49TH PARALLEL

I t is conceivable that the current unity struggle and constitutional uncertainty in Canada could provoke a deterioration in Canada-U.S. bilateral economic relations. Wholesale constitutional revisions might be exciting to political scientists, but many Canadians now fear that the constitutional talks have opened Pandora's box. Because Canada is the largest foreign market for U.S. goods, services, direct investment, and tourism, American policymakers in both the public and private sectors must be alert to the potential downside risks associated with Canada's domestic malaise. At least seven major problems could arise from Canada's unity and constitutional battles.

1. A newly independent Quebec nation could suffer a major economic downturn. At least in the short term, a sovereign Quebec would likely experience a drop in the production of goods and services. The new country would have a population base below seven million, appreciably smaller than the state of New Jersey's. Furthermore, Quebec's population would most likely decrease from its current level as tens of thousands of Anglophones exit the Francophone-dominated nation, resulting in a debilitating brain drain. Quebec companies and farmers would also lose access to some of their traditional markets in Canada. Moreover, the new Quebec government would stagger under added debt obligations, a damaged economy, and shattered consumer confidence. Consequently,

U.S. business affiliates in Quebec could face shrinking markets and higher tax burdens.

2. A new Canadian nation consisting of nine provinces also could suffer from economic stagnation. Even with the loss of Quebec, Canada would survive as a nation for the foreseeable future. Its fragmented market would be reduced to twenty million consumers, only slightly larger than the population base of New York or Texas. It too would suffer through an economic downturn, although not as severe as Quebec's. A new constitution would have to be drafted, and Canadians would face a period of political and economic uncertainty, a situation that could adversely affect business linkages between Canada and the United States.

3. A new constitutional arrangement could preserve the confederation but add billions of dollars to Ottawa's huge debt obligations. Ottawa, Quebec City, and the other provincial governments may finally succeed in drafting a constitutional document to preserve the Canadian confederation, but in the process drain billions of dollars from the national treasury. The added costs of aboriginal government, the transfer of responsibilities to provincial governments, and a host of new programs could threaten Ottawa's fiscal integrity. In turn, this could lead to higher interest rates, higher inflation, and higher taxes for individuals and corporations alike.

4. A devolution in powers could result in new trade barriers, regulations, and taxes being imposed by provincial and aboriginal governments. A devolution of major new responsibilities to provincial governments, the creation of scores of new aboriginal governments, and the failure to establish a true economic union from the Atlantic to the Pacific to the Arctic could provoke the dangerous fragmentation of the Canadian marketplace. U.S. subsidiaries could be subjected by these subnational government units to additional trade and investment barriers, discriminatory government procurement codes, new layers of regulations, and increased taxes. The need to adapt products and services to standards imposed by the ten provincial governments, two territorial governments, and perhaps dozens of aboriginal governments would greatly reduce Canada's attractiveness as a trade and investment partner for the United States.

5. The creation of a more powerful upper chamber in Parliament could promote political gridlock and greatly reduce the policymaking authority of the prime minister and the government. The establishment of an elected Senate with enhanced powers is a major departure from the British-inspired parliamentary system based on one dominant legislative chamber under the direction of a prime minister and a cabinet. The prime minister would have little control over the activities of the revamped Senate. Moreover, a hostile Senate majority, representing collectively as little as 13 percent of Canada's total population, could attempt to block government initiatives without having to formulate its own set of alternative policies. The resulting deadlock would do little to enhance a sense of Canadian nationhood and could seriously erode the confidence of the business community in national political institutions. Many Americans resent the gridlock in Washington, D.C., attributable in part to a White House headed by one political party and a Congress headed by the other major party. Canada may be in the process of replicating this gridlock by superimposing a more powerful Senate on its traditional parliamentary framework.

6. Constitutional and unity discussions could drag on for months or years, with the attendant uncertainty helping to prolong Canada's recession. If the results of the national referendum scheduled for October 26, 1992, are inconclusive, constitutional and unity discussions could conceivably drag on for months or even years. The lingering uncertainty might prolong Canada's economic stagnation and promote capital flight, a brain drain, a further fall in real estate values, and higher interest rates as the major financial centers around the world lose confidence in Ottawa's capacity to govern.[1] These conditions could result in Canada being the least desirable market within the nations comprising the Group of Seven (Canada, France, Germany, Japan, Italy, United Kingdom, and the United States).

7. Brian Mulroney's party could lose the next election, resulting in a new government opposed to the Canada-U.S. Free Trade Agreement (FTA) and the proposed North American Free Trade Agreement (NAFTA). The Mulroney government has fared very poorly in recent public opinion polls. Most Canadians are also disenchanted with the FTA and show little enthusiasm for the proposed tripartite agreement between Canada, the United States, and Mexico. In addition, both major opposition parties in Ottawa are on record calling either for the outright abrogation of the FTA or reopening the FTA negotiations in order to secure substantial new benefits for Canada. With the distinct possibility that a new government will take office in Ottawa in 1993, U.S. companies operating in Canada should prepare contingency plans based on the termination of the FTA or, at the least, significant revisions in the bilateral trade agreement.

PLANNING FOR BOTH WORST
AND BEST POSSIBLE OUTCOMES

Thus far, the 1990s have been a "lost" decade for many Canadians. Most have seen their standard of living stagnate or even decline. Many are turned off by the seemingly never-ending constitutional and unity squabbles. Some are very pessimistic about their futures and about the outlook for their country.

Whether they recognize it or not, many Americans also have a stake in Canada's future. A strong, united, economically robust Canada has long been taken for granted by its neighbors to the south. Even with the recent economic downturn, U.S. merchandise exports to Canada reached a record $85 billion in 1991.

The most pessimistic outlook would have Canada falling apart in a very acrimonious manner, or being constantly on the verge of disintegrating from within. The political realm would be traumatized by an inefficient policymaking process and by the virulent demands and protestations of Quebec, the other provincial governments, and various special interest groups. The economy would remain in the doldrums, provincial-level protectionism would proliferate, and Canada would withdraw from the FTA. Both Canadian and foreign investors would look elsewhere for much more hospitable business environments. Under these conditions, U.S. economic ties to Canada would fall back to levels of a decade or even two decades ago, jeopardizing hundreds of U.S. businesses and tens of thousands of American jobs.

The most probable outlook would have Canada maintaining national unity and reaching a tenuous consensus on constitutional revisions. Neither the unity nor constitutional demands would disappear, but other issues, particularly economic ones, would move to the top of the national agenda. Canada would remain a part of the FTA and would join the NAFTA once this tripartite pact has been ratified by the U.S. Congress. Trade and investment linkages between the United States and Canada would continue to grow, albeit at modest levels. The number of Canadian visitors to the United States might decline somewhat as the Canadian dollar weakens and Canadian retailers become more competitive.

The most optimistic outlook would involve a massive Quebec vote in favor of renewed federalism and widespread acceptance across Canada of a new constitutional package, a package that enhances Canada's economic union and makes few demands on the national treasury.

Canada's economic recovery would also pick up steam, with a big assist from the FTA and the NAFTA. A reinvigorated Canadian confederation and Canadian economy would result in expanded bilateral economic linkages and rapid job creation on both sides of the four-thousand mile-long border.

Ultimately, the people of Quebec will decide if their province remains a part of the confederation, and Canadians in general will decide the other major issues. The United States is simply a bystander as the sovereign Canadian people determine their own fates. Nevertheless, decision makers in the executive branch, on Capitol Hill, and in many corporate headquarters throughout the United States have a vested interest in the fate of Canada. In reference to the vast difference in size of the two neighboring economies, Canadians are fond of saying that when the United States sneezes, Canada usually catches a cold. Likewise, a critically ill Canada is capable of contaminating the U.S. economy, and spreading a harmful virus.

CHAPTER THREE

THE CONSTITUTIONAL CRISIS

C anada extends from the Atlantic to the Pacific, and from the U.S. border to the Arctic, spanning a total of six time zones. It is the world's second largest nation in land mass, about 60 percent the size of the new Russian Republic. The country is divided into ten provinces and two territories, with a third territory, Nunavut, the homeland of the Inuit (Eskimos), expected to be carved out of the existing Northwest Territories by the end of the decade.

In terms of human habitation, Canada's large geographic size is somewhat deceiving. Much of the area is inhospitable to human habitation, with over half of the land subject to permafrost (permanently frozen ground) and almost 90 percent having no permanent settlements.[1] Consequently, over two-thirds of Canadians are clustered within one hundred miles of the Canada-U.S. border, and three-quarters live in urban areas with populations exceeding fifty thousand. Canada's population of 27.5 million is slightly more than one-tenth the size of the United States and smaller than California's. Therefore, the second largest country geographically ranks as only the thirty-third most populated nation in the world.

Yet in spite of its small population base, Canada ranks as the seventh largest economy in the world and is a member of the exclusive Group of Seven, even though it has less than one-half the number of people to be found in the next most sparsely populated country, France. Its per-capita income is also among the highest in the world, and when measured in terms of purchasing power parity (PPP—what the average paycheck will buy in terms of a basket of goods and services), Canada ranks second only to the United States.

Thus, for the highly affluent Canadian people, the 1990s represent both the best of times and the worst of times. The United Nations recently selected Canada from among 160 countries as the "most liveable" nation in the world in terms of economic prosperity, living standards, distribution of income, human freedom, life expectancy, racial and gender equality, and other factors.[2] Undoubtedly, many people from around the planet would welcome the opportunity to move to Canada and to become citizens of what has often been referred to as the "peaceable kingdom."

Conversely, the recession of the 1990s has been more severe for Canada than for the United States, and the unity crisis adds another major layer of uncertainty to Canada's future prospects. As Keith Spicer, chairman of the Citizen's Forum on Canada's Future, has noted: "Seen from abroad, Canada looks like paradise. Seen from within, Canada looks to some Canadians like a pessimist's nightmare of Hell."[3] Echoing some of these sentiments, Allan Taylor, chairman of the Royal Bank of Canada, laments that his country is headed on "a march of folly" because so many people perceive Quebec's separation as a cure-all for Canada's ills, instead of regarding separation as a devastating loss both for Quebec and the rest of Canada (ROC).[4] As for average Canadians, they are basically fed up with the current political and constitutional debates, considering that these debates have gone on ad nauseum and are detracting from the urgent need to solve Canada's pressing economic problems. Allan Gregg recently told an Americas Society audience in New York City that he has never seen in thirteen years of polling a Canadian public so cynical, rudderless, and full of hopelessness. He added that the "public is not willing to let the government manage a two-hole outhouse."[5]

Although many residents of Quebec have long had reservations about their province's place in the Canadian confederation, the current unity debate was triggered originally by the victory of the Parti Québécois in the Quebec provincial elections of November 1976. The following outlines the major events leading up to the current constitutional and unity crises and will help to explain why so many Canadians are disenchanted and have developed an acute case of malaise.

The 1976 PQ Victory in the Provincial Elections. The PQ's primary campaign issue was a denunciation of the alleged corruption and inefficiencies of the previous government led by the Liberal party. However, the PQ platform also called for the creation of an independent Quebec nation through democratic means. This represented the first time that a government had been elected in Canada that was devoted to the secession of one of the original provinces that had formed the Canadian confederation back in 1867.

The May 1980 Quebec Referendum. The PQ government under the leadership of René Lévesque finally held its referendum in 1980 and asked the Quebec voters to authorize negotiations with Ottawa for "sovereignty-association," that is, political sovereignty combined with economic association with the rest of Canada. The issue was soundly defeated by a vote of 59 percent to 41 percent, with Francophones about equally split and with Anglophones and Allophones (those speaking neither French nor English as their first language) voting overwhelmingly against the proposal.

The referendum issue failed because Lévesque could not convince enough voters that their standard of living would not tumble precipitously if they opted for sovereignty-association. Moreover, Canadian Prime Minister Pierre Trudeau, also a native son of Quebec, had pledged to improve Quebec's status in the confederation if the electorate voted no. Although having spent a great deal of money in the United States in an effort to convince the business community that nothing substantive would change under sovereignty-association, the PQ government botched this public relations campaign. Lévesque made a disastrous speech at the Economic Club of New York in January 1977, and American business representatives worried about the ramifications of a "socialist" Quebec nation that would stay out of NATO and NORAD and maintain a "neutral" foreign policy.

PQ Reelection in April 1981. Despite the failure of its 1980 referendum, the PQ was returned to power in the 1981 provincial elections. This may be explained in part by the Quebec electorate's propensity of wanting to be well represented in the governing party in Ottawa while maintaining in power a strong advocate of provincial rights in Quebec City. In the federal elections, the voters continued to support Trudeau and his Liberal party, even though Trudeau was a dyed-in-the-wool centralist. Provincially, the voters opted for the PQ, which continued to advocate greater autonomy for Quebec but had temporarily suspended its quest for independence. Trudeau's pledge to invoke a new Charter of Rights and Freedoms meant that some provincial powers might be curtailed, so the Quebec voters wanted a strong defender of Quebec's rights running the National Assembly in Quebec City.

The Constitution Act, 1982. Trudeau was finally successful in "patriating" Canada's constitution (meaning that future constitutional amendments would no longer have to be ratified by the British Parliament) and in implementing the new Charter of Rights and Freedoms.

To fully understand this process of patriation, one must remember that Canada's quest for independence from Great Britain was peaceful and evolutionary, in marked contrast to the experience of England and the United States. In the domestic policy arena, Canada achieved a high degree of independence when the British Parliament approved the British North America Act in 1867 (now referred to as the Constitution Act, 1867). However, total control over foreign policy was not achieved until the proclamation in London of the 1931 Statute of Westminster. Even then, Canada's court of final appeal remained until 1949 Great Britain's Judicial Committee of the Privy Council. It was not until 1965 that the Maple Leaf replaced a version of the British Union Jack as Canada's official flag, and in 1980 "O Canada" officially replaced "God Save the Queen" as Canada's national anthem. Canada is indisputably an independent country, but attachments to the Commonwealth and the monarchy remain a fact of life north of the 49th parallel. Thus, most Canadians, with the possible exception of the Francophone community in Quebec, felt honored to have their queen and Canada's official head of state, Elizabeth II, travel to Ottawa and preside over Canada's 125th birthday celebration on July 1, 1992.

In the aftermath of Quebec's referendum on sovereignty-association, Trudeau announced in October 1980 that it was time to "patriate" Canada's constitution, meaning that Canada would no longer ask the British Parliament for final ratification of amendments to the Constitution Act, 1867. Even more importantly, Trudeau pledged to add a bill of rights to Canada's constitution, insisting that this would rejuvenate Canada's troubled system of federalism and promote a stronger sense of Canadian nationhood.

Prior to Trudeau's announcement, thirteen constitutional conferences had been held over a period of more than a half century without any notable achievements. The major stumbling block to success was in attaining unanimous support from the federal government and all of the provincial governments. More specifically, the Quebec government had been responsible for blocking several of the most recent attempts to implement a revised constitutional amendment formula.

After months of difficult and acrimonious negotiations in 1981,

Trudeau and nine provincial premiers finally accepted a new constitutional package that included an amending formula, a Charter of Rights and Freedoms, and several other changes in the Constitution Act, 1867. However, Lévesque considered the new constitutional arrangement to be a betrayal of Quebec, and Quebec's National Assembly refused to endorse the package. Trudeau then proceeded to implement the new Constitution Act, 1982, without Quebec's approval, claiming that the previous practice of unanimous consent was simply a custom and had no legal standing. Canada's Supreme Court eventually ruled in favor of Trudeau's position. On April 17, 1982, while Queen Elizabeth II was signing the new Constitution Act on Parliament Hill in Ottawa, René Lévesque was proclaiming the day as one of the bleakest in Quebec's history.

Mulroney's Victory, 1984. Brian Mulroney and his Progressive Conservative party won a landslide victory in the national election of September 1984, which was helped immensely by the Quebec voters' defection from the Liberal party and their willingness to support native-son Mulroney and his Conservative slate of candidates. In contrast to former Prime Minister Trudeau, Mulroney promised to support selective decentralization and to work with Quebec's leadership to win acceptance of the 1982 constitutional package.

Bourassa's Victory, 1985. Robert Bourassa and his Quebec Liberal party decisively defeated the PQ in the provincial elections held in December 1985. Bourassa stated that he was willing to work with Mulroney in piecing together a package that would finally secure Quebec's approval of the Constitution Act, 1982.

1987 Meech Lake Accord. At the Meech Lake resort located near Ottawa, Mulroney and the ten provincial premiers unanimously supported a new constitutional package that Bourassa asserted would satisfy his five pivotal constitutional demands: (1) formal recognition of Quebec as a distinct society; (2) a Quebec veto over future constitutional change involving federal institutions; (3) expanded Quebec participation in the nomination of Supreme Court judges; (4) an enhanced Quebec role in the selection of immigrants; and (5) strict limits on the use of federal spending powers within areas of provincial jurisdiction.

The 1988 FTA Election. Departing from customary practices, the Canadian Senate forced Mulroney to call for new parliamentary elections in November 1988, claiming that the FTA with the United States required the approval of the Canadian voters. The Conservatives were returned to power with a reduced majority, and the FTA went into effect on January 1, 1989. Quebec was once again the key contributor to the Conservatives' success and offered among the strongest support in Canada for the FTA.

The 1989 Bill 178 Controversy. French became the "official" language of Quebec in 1974 after the passage of Bill 22 in Quebec's National Assembly, and official unilingualism was strengthened in 1977 with the passage of Bill 101. In December 1988, the Supreme Court of Canada overturned some of the provisions in Bill 101, claiming they were in violation of the new Charter of Rights and Freedoms. Bourassa's government countered by passing Bill 178, invoking Canada's peculiar "notwithstanding" clause (Section 33 of the Constitution Act, 1982 permitting provincial governments to place in abeyance the enforcement of certain Supreme Court decisions regarding the Charter). Bill 178 outlawed the use of English on outdoor signs and mandated that English have a subordinate status in indoor advertising. Many people in the rest of Canada were infuriated with Bourassa's decision, perceiving that the Quebec Francophone majority was being unfair to the Anglophone minority and was ignoring basic individual freedoms guaranteed by Canada's bill of rights. Bourassa's action hardened opposition in the ROC to the distinct society and veto provisions in the Meech Lake accord.

The 1990 Failure of Meech Lake. Because of proposed changes in Canada's constitutional amendment formula, the 1987 Meech Lake agreement required that the federal Parliament and all ten provincial legislatures ratify the accord within a three-year period. However, following the consensus reached in 1987, changes in government were to occur in New Brunswick, Newfoundland, and Manitoba. These new governments demanded substantial modifications in the accord, and after the dust had settled, Meech Lake failed to gain the approval of the Newfoundland and Manitoba legislatures (together representing only 6 percent of Canada's population) before the June 1990 deadline.

In spite of the fact that the Meech Lake accord was ratified by the Parliament and eight provincial legislatures, many Canadians harbored serious reservations about the constitutional package. They perceived that the proposed distinct society clause and the constitutional veto provision would mean that the residents of Quebec would be treated better than other Canadian citizens, and that the Quebec government would hold powers denied to governments in the other nine provinces, creating an asymmetrical federal system. Some were also fed up with Quebec's constant demand for greater powers, insisting that Quebec was already accorded special privileges within the confederation. For example, Quebec continued to have the same number of senators as Ontario, even though Ontario's population base was over 40 percent larger than Quebec's. Moreover, three of the nine judges on the Supreme Court must come from the Quebec bar and be trained in Quebec's civil code rather than the common-law system used elsewhere in Canada. Furthermore, since the end of World War II, residents of Quebec have served as Canada's prime minister for more than 70 percent of the period. Thus, rather than perceiving Quebec's Francophone population as being subjected to the rules and regulations mandated by Canada's Anglophone majority, many people in the ROC viewed the Francophones as being a privileged group whose constant demands were excessive and could never be satisfied.

Quebec's Reaction to Meech Lake's Rejection, 1990-91. Disappointed and infuriated with the rejection of the Meech Lake package, Bourassa vowed to boycott future constitutional meetings and to ensure that the Quebec voters would have the final say in determining Quebec's political future. He authorized the Quebec Liberal party to draft a document on Quebec's future. This document, known as the Allaire Report, was approved at the Liberal party's biennial convention in March 1991. It took a tough stance on the unity issue, demanding that if Quebec were to remain in confederation, twenty-two powers must be transferred from Ottawa to Quebec. The all-party Bélanger-Campeau Commission on Quebec's Future called for a referendum to be held either on the issue of sovereignty or renewed federalism and suggested that the economic costs of sovereignty for the Quebec people would be minimal. If the Quebec electorate were to opt for the sovereignty option, the Bélanger-Campeau Commission recommended that Quebec seek such a status within one year of the referendum vote. The PQ, under the leadership of Jacques Parizeau, demanded that Quebec seek outright political independence while maintaining close economic relations with the rest of Canada. Eventually, Premier Bourassa opted to articulate a more conciliatory position, asking that Mulroney and the nine provincial premiers elsewhere in Canada agree on a renewed federalism package that would convince Quebec voters to remain a part of Canada.

Bill 150 was enacted by the National Assembly in June 1991, requiring that a referendum on sovereignty be held by no later than October 26, 1992. Two committees were also formed, one to examine the sovereignty option for Quebec and the other to analyze the merits of any renewed federalism package that would be presented by the rest of Canada. These committees would present their findings and recommendations prior to the October referendum.

Mulroney's 1991 Constitutional Proposals. In response to Quebec's decision to hold a referendum, Prime Minister Mulroney presented in September 1991 a report entitled "Canada's Future Together." This report included twenty-eight "unity" proposals that, if implemented, would drastically change Canada's system of government. The Senate would be totally revamped, with senators elected by provincial constituencies with an "equitable" distribution of seats among the provinces and the two federal territories. A new Council of the Federation would coordinate policies between the federal and provincial governments. Ottawa would transfer the residual powers to the provinces and turn over a number of functions to these noncentral governments. On the other hand, Ottawa would centralize economic policies to ensure the free flow of goods, services, capital, and labor within Canada. Finally, Quebec would be recognized as a distinct society in terms of language, culture, and civil law.

Prior to the release of this report, other committees and commissions at both the federal and provincial levels met with individuals and representatives of interest groups to explore new arrangements for Canada. This strategy was followed in part as a reaction to bitter criticism that the Meech Lake process had been secretive and exclusionary, involving only eleven white men in business suits. In particular, the Citizens' Forum on Canada's Future, headed by Keith Spicer, held unstructured public discussions for several months in an effort to determine the aspirations and concerns of people and groups from throughout Canada. Over three hundred thousand Canadians provided comments to the forum, which submitted its final report in June 1991. This report emphasized that Canadians were very unhappy with the leadership provided by the Mulroney government and were willing to experiment with a much more Americanized political system.

The ROC's Constitutional Deliberations, 1991-92. The Dobbie-Beaudoin Committee, composed of twenty members of the House of Commons and ten members of the Senate representing all three major political parties, was set up to examine Mulroney's unity proposals and to recommend a renewed-federalism package. The committee got off to a rocky start, but eventually met with representatives in all of the provinces and then sponsored a series of major constitutional forums across Canada. At the end of February 1992, the Dobbie-Beaudoin Committee presented an extensive list of recommendations for political, economic, and constitutional reform. The reaction of the Bourassa government to these recommendations was lukewarm at best, and PQ leader Parizeau rejected them out of hand, claiming that they fell far short of the five minimum conditions that Quebec had demanded during the Meech Lake process.

Between March and June 1992, Minister for Constitutional Affairs Joe Clark sponsored "multilateral discussions" with representatives of the federal government, the nine provincial governments (Quebec continued to boycott all such meetings), the two territorial governments (the Yukon and the Northwest Territories), and four aboriginal groups (Status Indians, non-Status Indians, Métis, and the Inuit). These discussions were suspended in June without reaching a final package of proposals. Major stumbling blocks included the reform of the Senate and a constitutional veto for Quebec over changes in federal institutions. Representatives from four provinces, led by Alberta and Newfoundland, insisted that Canada must have a Triple-E Senate that would be elected, effective, and equal (each province would have the same number of seats). The Triple-E Senate would have much in common with the U.S. Senate, although it would have fewer powers than the other parliamentary chamber, the House of Commons. However, in matters that touch on provincial jurisdiction, nothing could be passed without the approval of the Senate. Backers of the Triple-E Senate insisted that discussions on a constitutional veto for Quebec could not be concluded until a package on Senate reform had been passed; otherwise, a Quebec veto power would permit it to block all future reform of the Senate and other federal institutions.

On June 29, 1992, Prime Minister Mulroney called the nine premiers to Ottawa for a luncheon meeting. He stated that if a consensus could not be reached on a renewed-federalism package, he would call Parliament back into session on July 15 and present for ratification the federal government's own package of reforms. He also suggested that a national referendum might be held to seek the direct approval of the Canadian people, an option fraught with danger because of the unpopularity of the Mulroney government and the qualms of many people in the ROC concerning making further concessions to Quebec.

In an effort to beat the July 15 deadline, Clark and the nine provincial premiers met in Ottawa in early July and were successful in reaching agreement on a tentative constitutional package. Nevertheless, many residents of Quebec were very unhappy with parts of the proposed package, and even some of the premiers in the rest of Canada began to have some second thoughts about certain provisions.

However, this tentative agreement was sufficient to convince Robert Bourassa to end his boycott of constitutional meetings and to return to the bargaining table. After several days of discussions involving federal, provincial, territorial, and aboriginal representatives, a new constitutional accord was drafted and later approved by all negotiating parties at Charlottetown on August 28. Some of the highlights include:

1. Recognition of Quebec as a "distinct society" in terms of language, culture, and its civil code. This recognition would be included in the so-called Canada Clause where it could be used by the court system in interpreting the entire constitution.
2. The creation of a new Senate with six senators from each province and one from each territory, with each provincial and territorial government deciding how its senators will be selected. A majority of senators would be able to kill any bill dealing with the taxation of natural resources. Otherwise, a rejection of a bill by the Senate would lead to a joint sitting of the House of Commons and the Senate, with each member allowed one vote. Any Senate bills dealing with language and culture would require a double majority—a majority of senators plus a majority of Francophone senators.
3. The House of Commons would be expanded from 295 to 337 seats, with Ontario and Quebec each gaining 18 new seats, British Columbia 4, and Alberta 2. Quebec would be guaranteed, in perpetuity, 25 percent of the seats in the House of Commons, regardless of its future share of Canada's total population.
4. Aboriginals would be accorded the inherent right to self-government, with a five-year waiting period before disputes could be referred to the court system. No new land rights would be recognized as a result of this accord, and native laws must conform with federal and provincial laws in matters related to "peace, order, and good government."
5. The federal and provincial governments agreed in principle to remove interprovincial trade barriers.
6. Each provincial government would be granted veto power over constitutional amendments dealing with federal institutions and would be given a limited voice in the process leading to the creation of new provinces.

7. Provincial governments could demand a transfer of powers from Ottawa and assume control of policies related to forestry, mining, tourism, recreation, housing, and municipal and urban affairs. The provinces would also control most aspects of culture and of labor market training, and could request added responsibilities in immigration matters and regional economic development.

This agreement represents a significant step forward in the unity and constitutional debate, but many obstacles must still be hurdled. Above all, the people of Quebec must approve this new constitutional package. Quebeckers have long feared that they will lose clout in Ottawa as their share of Canada's population dwindles. Under the proposed agreement, their proportion of Senate seats will diminish from about one-quarter to less than one-tenth, even though the Francophone members will be able to veto proposed legislation dealing with language and culture, and Quebec will be granted 25 percent of the seats in the House of Commons.

Another major stumbling block may be found in the wording of the final constitutional package and the costs involved in implementing the package. Some of the concepts have not been adequately defined, including aboriginal self-government, a proposed social charter, economic union, the new division of powers, and so on. Once Canadians see the final text and are shown the final price tag, they may have serious reservations about certain parts of the package.

The third major hurdle will be the ratification process itself. Most of the package must be approved using the "7-50" formula: the approval of the Canadian Parliament and at least seven provinces representing more than 50 percent of the national population. The change in the constitutional amending formula dealing with federal institutions will require unanimous approval by Ottawa and the ten provinces. All of the provinces have agreed to hold a referendum on October 26, 1992, to approve the proposed constitutional package. Quebec will proceed with its own referendum on the same date under rules stipulated by Quebec's National Assembly. If one province other than Quebec rejects the package, the section dealing with vetoing future changes in federal institutions will apparently be null and void because of the failure to achieve unanimity. On the other hand, if Quebec's voters reject the constitutional package while the electorate in the other nine provinces approve it, the schism between Quebec and the ROC may be more profound than ever before. Thus, when one places the entire process in perspective, the Charlottetown agreement reached between Brian Mulroney, Joe Clark, and the provincial, territorial, and aboriginal representatives on August 28, 1992, is undoubtedly of critical importance for Canada's future. Nevertheless, the journey ahead remains very arduous, and there is still a possibility that the constitutional accord will not be ratified by the requisite number of provinces. Moreover, even if all ten provinces support the package in October, one must anticipate that future Quebec governments will continue to demand modifications resulting in the transfer of additional policy-making authority to Quebec City.

CHAPTER FOUR

THE QUEBEC DIMENSION

Premier Robert Bourassa has consistently favored the option that would permit Quebec to remain in Canada, as long as the ROC approves the five minimum conditions that he presented at the Meech Lake conference. If the people of Quebec are to vote in a referendum, Bourassa prefers that the question deal with a renewed federalism package supported by the ROC rather than the issue of outright sovereignty or sovereignty-association.

Anywhere from 40 to 50 percent of the Quebec electorate apparently favor some form of sovereignty, although tactically, some may simply voice support for sovereignty in order to win concessions from Ottawa and the ROC. In his testimony before the Bélanger-Campeau Commission, Professor Léon Dion outlined the utility of such a strategy. He asserted that Quebec must threaten separation in order to provoke an interest from the ROC, adding that "English Canada will not make concessions . . . unless it has a knife to its throat."[1] Moreover, the Quebeckers' perception of what sovereignty entails is somewhat cloudy. Some believe that Quebec can be sovereign and still elect members to the Canadian Parliament, carry the Canadian passport, use the Canadian currency, and continue to trade freely with the ROC. Prime Minister Brian Mulroney has done his best to clarify the issue for Quebec voters, insisting that a vote for sovereignty would be a vote for complete separation from Canada and for the creation of an independent Quebec nation-state. He added that sovereignty is not a cafeteria where the voters choose what sort of linkages they would maintain or cut off with the ROC.

PQ leader Jacques Parizeau has also muddied the waters, insisting that citizens in a sovereign Quebec would retain the right to use the Canadian currency and passport and to trade with the rest of Canada. According to the PQ, citizenship in an independent Quebec would be offered to Canadians living in Quebec at the moment of independence, and to those born outside of Quebec but whose parents were once Quebec residents. Parizeau has also promised a government job to every federal civil servant living in Quebec at the time of independence, effectively doubling the size of Quebec's public bureaucracy.[2] Quebec would also maintain its own armed forces, sign international treaties, and join the United Nations, NATO, and NORAD. It would collect its own taxes and customs duties, and unless an FTA were agreed to by Quebec and the ROC, duties would also be collected on goods emanating from the ROC.[3]

Why are so many people in Quebec tempted by the sovereignty option? Undoubtedly, the creation of new nations in Eastern Europe, particularly the proposed establishment of separate Slovak and Czech republics, has prompted some Quebeckers to believe that the time is ripe for Quebec to go its own way. But the roots of discontent are far deeper than the rush for sovereignty occurring elsewhere in the world.

Since the fall of New France to the British in 1759, French-speaking Canadians have often perceived themselves as second-class citizens on an English-dominated continent. In actuality, the British were willing to recognize Francophones as a distinct society in the Quebec Act of 1774, granting religious freedom and the right to retain their language and civil code. Nonetheless, tensions between Francophones and Anglophones continued to grow as more English-speaking people came to North America. Following a series of rebellions in Quebec (then known as Lower Canada), the British government dispatched Lord Durham to investigate. Lord Durham emphasized that he found "two nations warring in the bosom of a single state," and his 1839 report recommended that the two colonies of Upper and Lower Canada be merged into one, that responsible government be created, and that French Canadians be assimilated into the English system. The first two recommendations were implemented, but assimilation was not adopted as official policy. Nonetheless, Francophones have long considered themselves as a small island in a sea of Anglophones, and that assimilation, whether officially sanctioned or not, would always remain a threat to their way of life.

Today, 83 percent of Quebec's population of 6.8 million are Francophones, but until the 1960s the Anglophone minority dominated the business sector. In 1961, the average English Quebecker earned 51 percent more than a French Quebecker.[4] Non-Francophones also owned 78 percent of assets in the manufacturing sector and 74 percent in the financial sector.[5] A turning point in modern Quebec history occurred in June 1960 when Jean Lesage became the premier and dedicated his government to modernizing Quebec society and permitting the Francophone majority to be "maître chez nous" (masters of our own house). The ensuing Quiet Revolution permitted talented Francophones to achieve success within the public sector, a sector that was expanded dramatically to include ownership in a wide variety of business ventures. This spurred in turn the development of Quebec Inc., an informal partnership between the government, business, and labor. The pillars of Quebec Inc. include (1) extensive state ownership, especially in the resource and energy sectors; (2) the Caisse de dépôt et placement du Québec, a $35 billion pension fund, which is the largest single investor in Canadian equities and which specializes in funding Quebec-based enterprises; (3) the Quebec Federation of Labor's Solidarity Fund, a $280 million venture-capital fund; (4) and the Société de développement industriel (SDI), a Quebec agency which is a lender of last resort to the corporate sector.[6] In addition, Francophones tend to place their savings in the Desjardins credit union movement. This savings institution uses a good share of its $44 billion in assets to promote economic development in Quebec.

Some of Quebec Inc.'s recent ventures have gone sour, either going into bankruptcy (Lavalin) or losing record amounts of money (Domtar). Nonetheless, the Francophone business sector is more confident than ever before, and Quebec's business schools are cranking out far more MBAs proportionally than anywhere else in Canada. Unlike the 1960s or even the 1970s, Francophones now control the levers of power in the business sector, accounting for over 80 percent of management positions.[7] Yet they may still be overly dependent on the largess of the Francophone-dominated provincial government. In effect, many in the business community, as well as Francophones in general, perceive that the Quebec government should be the ultimate guarantor of their way of life and their standard of living.

Regardless of how the sovereignty issue fares in 1992 and 1993, it will not disappear. If anything, the Francophones' emotional attachment to the Quebec state is stronger than ever before. That is not to say that many do not have positive feelings toward Canada, but the attachment in this case may be more economic than emotional. Ottawa helps to provide Francophones with one of the highest standards of living in the world. Quebec City, on the other hand, is the ultimate source of protection for the language, the culture, the legal system, and the overall way of life in a country where Quebec once represented 36 percent of Canada's population but will represent less than 25 percent at the turn of the century.[8]

Unlike in the United States, Canada's principal minority group is concentrated in one geographic area, the province of Quebec, where it enjoys a massive majority. About 85 percent of all Francophones in Canada reside in Quebec, and two-thirds of these people speak little if any English.[9] With the exception of neighboring New Brunswick, Francophones represent less than 4 percent of the population in each of the other provinces, even though the 1969 Official Languages Act proclaimed Canada as an officially bilingual country.[10] In several provinces, Francophones do not even constitute the major minority language group, and most provinces have experienced a downward trend in Francophone representation. At one time, some Francophones thought that "la revanche des berceaux" (revenge of the cradles) would ensure that they would continue to be a major part of the overall Canadian population. In 1957, for example, Quebec had one of the highest birthrates in the world, with more than four children per woman of childbearing age. But in the 1980s and the 1990s, after years of urbanization, modernization, and secularization, the birthrate has fallen to among the lowest levels in the world and is now below the level of zero population growth.[11] Nevertheless, the Quebec government has not abandoned the cradle option, providing significant financial incentives for large families. In addition to free medical care, families with one child receive a bonus of $500 (C), with a second child $1,000 (C), and with a third and each subsequent child $8,000 (C). Childcare allowances have also been increased substantially.

In the Meech Lake discussions, the Quebec government also pushed for control over immigration, insisting that this represented another way of guaranteeing that Francophones would remain a solid majority in the province. Ottawa has now relinquished some control over immigration to Quebec, permitting the provincial government to station its own immigration officers overseas and to screen "independent" immigrants (those without family already in Canada and those not claiming a refugee status) desiring to settle in Quebec. Canada is now welcoming almost

250,000 immigrants per year, and Quebec has been assured that it will receive about 25 percent of these new arrivals.[12] Quebec's aim is to attract Francophones or those willing to learn the French language. The Quebec government also wants skilled immigrants who will help Quebec to compete effectively in the large North American marketplace. People from France have been a priority target for Quebec, and the government maintains a delegation office in Paris which actually employs more people than the Canadian Embassy. Unfortunately, about half of the recent arrivals from France have gone back home, complaining about the lack of job opportunities and difficulty in adapting to the Quebeckers' life-style.[13] Consequently, most of the new arrivals are coming from developing countries and are grateful for the opportunity to achieve prosperity in an advanced industrial society.

Conversely, immigrant groups that have arrived in Quebec over the past quarter century have serious reservations about the increasingly unilingual nature of Quebec society. The Charter of the French Language, Bill 101, was promulgated in 1977 and stipulates that French is the official language in Quebec. With very few exceptions, parents moving to Quebec must educate their children in the French language, in spite of the fact that English-language schools are readily available in major urban areas. Moreover, enterprises with more than fifty employees must conduct their business in French. All outdoor signs must also advertise in French, and although indoor signs can be in French and another language, the French lettering must be at least twice as large. In 1989, Bourassa's government also initiated a costly and somewhat embarrassing campaign to replace all "stop" signs with "arrêt" signs by 1993. A Commission de protection de la langue française has been established to enforce the provisions of Bill 101, Bill 178, and related laws, and critics often refer to its officers as the "tongue troopers." This criticism is generally unfair because officials at the commission tend to be quite pragmatic and attempt to avoid confrontations whenever possible. In particular, flexibility is shown to businesses willing to locate in Quebec and create jobs for local citizens. Nevertheless, French is the only official language in Quebec and the commission is charged with the responsibility of making sure that the language laws are respected.

Recent surveys indicate that few Allophones (those who speak a first language other than French or English) are supportive of the quest for sovereignty.[14] Many also complain that the enforcement of Bill 101 has been a deterrent to their mobility because business elsewhere in Canada is conducted in English. They argue that they are Canadians first and would appreciate the opportunity to be educated in either of Canada's two official languages, French or English. Before Bill 101 was implemented, the vast majority of immigrant groups opted to educate their children in English. Today, most immigrant children have no choice but to attend French schools. Because of these limited options, some immigrant families soon depart Quebec and move to other areas of Canada. This helps to explain why the Quebec government wants its own officers to screen potential immigrants, selecting those who have positive feelings about being educated in French and being a part of a Francophone-dominated business community.

Over the past quarter century, Quebec's English-speaking minority has also felt increasingly under siege, even though Francophones often observe that the English in Quebec are among the most affluent minorities in the entire world. At the time of confederation in 1867, English-speaking people were a majority in both Montreal and Quebec City and constituted about a quarter of the provincial population.[15] Now they are a distinct minority in these two metropolitan centers and their numbers are dwindling across the province. Approximately three-quarters of a million Anglophones currently reside in Quebec, representing about 11 percent of Quebec's population, but 120,000 have exited the province over the past fifteen years. More alarmingly, enrollment in English language public and private schools has dropped by 57 percent between 1972 and 1990, from 250,000 to 108,000.[16] Anglophones are also slightly underrepresented in the National Assembly, significantly underrepresented in the federal civil service in Quebec, and grossly underrepresented in the provincial civil service, holding only 1 percent of the jobs in this latter sector.[17] Although many Anglophones have lived in Quebec for generations, they maintain a strong emotional attachment to Canada and consider Quebec to be one of ten subnational jurisdictions within a united Canada. They applauded when both the Quebec Court of Appeal in December 1986 and the Canadian Supreme Court, in a unanimous decision announced in December 1988, ruled that some sections of Bill 101 violated the freedom-of-expression provisions in the Charter of Rights and Freedoms and thus were unconstitutional. They were in despair when Bourassa invoked the notwithstanding clause, placing the Supreme Court's decision in abeyance. They joined with Anglophones elsewhere in Canada in condemning Bill 178, which was passed hastily by the National Assembly just prior to the Christmas recess in 1988.

Although softening some of the provisions in Bill 101, Bill 178 continued to defy the ruling of Canada's Supreme Court and prohibited the use of English on outdoor signs.

Mordecai Richler, a native son of Montreal who readily admits that he is not fluent in French, has led the way in condemning what he considers to be the exclusionary policies of the Quebec government. He has also infuriated many Francophones and some prominent Jewish leaders by accusing French-speaking Quebeckers of being tribalistic and anti-Semitic, adding that the Jewish community in Montreal has shrunk from 120,000 to 95,000 over the past twenty years.[18] He laments that "just about everything has been done to make the Anglophone youth, even those who are fluently bilingual, feel unwelcome in Quebec."[19] Richler adds that "if there is a truly endangered species in Canada, it is the non-Francophone population of Quebec."[20]

Aboriginal groups are also a thorn in the side of Quebec's political leaders. In the summer of 1990, a small band of Mohawks near Montreal cut off access to disputed land, insisting that municipal and provincial authorities were not respecting the land claims and other rights of native groups. This precipitated a much-publicized standoff between the Mohawks on the one side and provincial and federal officers on the other, with one provincial police officer being killed during a confrontation. Many people across Canada seemed to sympathize with the Mohawk's position, whereas many in Quebec considered the band's actions as totally unlawful and their claims without sufficient merit.

To the far north, the Cree have been engaged in a campaign to halt the expansion of Hydro-Quebec's huge hydroelectric project along James Bay. The Cree claim that their way of life would be threatened by the so-called Great Whale project and that the land belongs to them. Hydro-Quebec officials counter by referring to the 1975 James Bay Agreement signed by representatives of the federal government, the Quebec government, the Cree, and the Inuit. This pact permits Hydro-Quebec to develop facilities in an area encompassing over one million square kilometers, larger than Germany, France, England, Belgium, and Luxembourg combined. In return, the seventeen thousand aboriginals in the area (10,500 Cree and 6,500 Inuit) have received guaranteed income support and improved health care and educational facilities. The children are also educated in their native language with either English or French as their second language.

The Cree argue that the Great Whale expansion is not covered by the original James Bay Agreement. Their representatives have appealed to

Ottawa to adopt federal legislation that would prevent Hydro-Quebec from developing the next phase of the massive hydroelectric project. They also hired public relations and legal experts and launched a publicity campaign in New York City and in the New England area in an effort to convince U.S. utilities to abandon plans to buy hydroelectricity from the James Bay project. Governor Mario Cuomo finally announced in March 1992 that New York would not proceed with a $14.5 billion contract to buy one thousand megawatts of electricity from Hydro-Quebec. Even though Cuomo's decision was based primarily on the price of hydroelectricity versus other forms of energy, the Cree claimed a major victory for aboriginals and for environmentalists.

Aboriginal groups throughout Quebec also insist that if Quebec separates from Canada, they should have the right to separate from Quebec or to remain a part of the ROC. Aboriginals have made ancestral claims at one time or another for about 85 percent of the land mass in Quebec, even though they represent about 1 percent of the province's total population.[21] Moreover, the vast northern region of Quebec, known as Ungava, was actually ceded to the province by the federal government in 1912, long after Quebec's admittance into confederation. Aboriginals claim much of this land, and some scholars in Quebec and elsewhere in Canada insist that this land should revert back to the control of Canada if Quebeckers opt for independence.[22] Sovereignty advocates scoff at these suggestions, insisting that an independent Quebec will maintain its current boundaries and that a settlement can be reached with aboriginal groups to provide them with self-government and with some territorial sovereignty.[23]

If a referendum on sovereignty is held in the foreseeable future, pro-independence forces will face a very stiff battle. The vast majority of Anglophones and Allophones will certainly vote against sovereignty, and aboriginal groups feel much more comfortable interacting with Ottawa than with Quebec City. The Quebec provincial government carries a debt load of $33 billion (C), state-owned Hydro-Quebec also has $30 billion (C) in outstanding debt, and an independent Quebec would be expected to assume the annual payments on somewhat less than one-quarter of the Canadian government's outstanding debt of $450 billion (C). Thus, the burden of interest payments would make it more difficult for Quebec City to invest in infrastructure and other related projects designed to help the fledgling nation compete in the North American and the global economies. In addition, it would most likely add to what is already a heavy tax burden carried by households and the corporate community.

Some businesses and farm groups also fear the loss of markets in Canada. For example, Quebec dairy farmers now supply about one-half of Canada's industrial milk at a guaranteed price. It is difficult to imagine that the ROC would permit these farmers continued access to its markets after sovereignty was proclaimed. The prospect of having to renegotiate parts of the Free Trade Agreement with Canada and the United States is also worrisome to some in the Quebec business community. Canada's chief FTA negotiator, Simon Reisman, has insisted that about half of the changes that Washington asked Canada to make during the FTA discussions were linked to Quebec's policies regarding investment restrictions, cultural protection, state-owned enterprises, subsidies, and government procurement codes.[24]

Quebec has also endured its most profound economic downturn since the Great Depression. The Montreal region, which celebrated its 350th anniversary in 1992 and is home to one-half of Quebec's total population, may now have the highest unemployment rate among major Canadian and U.S. cities, and over three hundred thousand of its residents live in poverty.[25] The commercial real estate market has also been in a deep slump, with almost 30 percent of commercial sites vacant.[26] Quebec Inc.'s reputation has also been somewhat tarnished because of numerous business failures and ill-conceived investments. The loss of the huge hydroelectric contract with the state of New York also raises doubts about the completion of the vast Great Whale project and places an additional burden on Hydro-Quebec in financing its burgeoning debt. Furthermore, most scholarly studies within Quebec and within Canada indicate that a sovereign Quebec will suffer a sizable economic downturn in the short and medium term, and that a substantial "brain drain" will occur as well-educated Anglophones and Allophones abandon Quebec. This brain drain would be especially acute for Quebec, because it suffers from the highest high school dropout rate in Canada.[27] In 1990-91, 36 percent of students dropped out of high school, compared with 27.5 percent in 1985-86. The most recent rate includes a staggering 42 percent of boys and 28 percent of girls.[28] The reasons for this high dropout rate are complex, linked to urbanization pressures, broken families, the difficulty experienced by recent immigrant groups in mastering the French language, and tough graduation standards. Moreover, it was not until the 1960s that access to secondary education in Quebec became a universal right, so the completion of a high school education is still a relatively recent phenomenon.[29]

If Quebec is to compete effectively continentally and globally, it must have a well-educated work force, and it is simply not producing the number of skilled graduates that it currently needs. With this and other issues in mind, a profederalist business lobby has been formed in Quebec, claiming a membership of twelve thousand. On May 20, 1992, Jean Campeau announced the formation of a pro-independence Quebec business group called Souveraineté Québec Inc., but this group is still very small in comparison with the profederalist business lobby.[30]

The influence of the Parti Québécois during the referendum campaign is also subject to some speculation. Currently, the people support the sovereignty option more than they support the PQ, and they support the PQ much more than they support PQ leader Jacques Parizeau. This is exactly the opposite of the conditions that existed in 1980 when the charismatic and widely admired René Lévesque directed the PQ government. Parizeau is an economics professor from the University of Montreal who has been a steady but unspectacular leader of the PQ. It is difficult for him to tug at the heartstrings of the Quebec people, at a time when it will be critical for the PQ, as an opposition party with only one-quarter of the seats in the National Assembly, to gain the emotional support of the Quebec electorate. In contrast, one can be assured that Robert Bourassa and his huge National Assembly majority will highlight a number of persuasive "pocketbook" issues illustrating why Quebec should remain within the Canadian confederation.

In the 1980 referendum, voters rejected the sovereignty-association option because they feared that their pocketbooks would be adversely affected, and they were not totally confident that Quebec's business community was prepared to go it alone. Since that referendum, there has been a tremendous upsurge in Francophone ownership in the business community and, in spite of the recession, a new confidence that Francophone businesses can be regionally and globally competitive. Moreover, Francophones are fairly confident that the Canada-U.S. Free Trade Agreement would be extended to an independent Quebec nation, and that the economic losses attributable to cutting off linkages with the ROC would be offset by Quebec's unimpaired access to the huge consumer market of two hundred fifty million people in the United States.

Nevertheless, the jury is still out on whether the Francophone community's strong emotional attachment to "l'état du Québec" will offset worries about a drop in its standard of living. Many are very sympathetic with the sovereigntists' argument that the only way to guarantee the viability of their language, culture, and way of life is to permit Quebec City to be the repository of all political and social powers. They recognize that Francophones represent only one-quarter of Canada's total population, and that this proportion is continuing to dwindle. They are generally supportive of the Trudeau-inspired Charter of Rights and Freedoms but are concerned that the protection of individual rights will erode the collective rights of the Francophone community in Quebec. They are fully cognizant of the fact that the levers of political power are exercised by Anglophone majorities in the House of Commons and the Senate, on Canada's Supreme Court, and around the table at the periodic meetings of the prime minister and the ten provincial premiers.

They are also swayed by the argument that the world is now dividing into regional trading blocs, and that whether Quebec is independent or not, it will be an integral part of the North American economy. Thus, in the long run, Quebec should do well economically, regardless of its status as an independent country or as one of ten provinces in Canada. Consequently, why not opt for sovereignty now and control one's own political destiny, while at the same time taking full advantage of a 360-million-member North American market, running from the Yukon to the Yucatan, with a combined annual gross domestic product exceeding $6.3 trillion.

In addition, the failure of Ottawa and the provincial and territorial governments to produce a plausible renewed federalism package would work to the advantage of the sovereigntists. Many Quebeckers already feel a deep sense of betrayal vis-à-vis the ROC. They refer to the evening in November 1981 when Trudeau's emissaries reached an agreement with the nine premiers on a new constitutional package, without the approval of René Lévesque, as the "night of the long knives." They also perceive the rejection of the Meech Lake accord in June 1990 as the second major example of Canada's Anglophone majority turning its back on Quebec. The submission by the ROC of a very shoddy renewed federalism package would be construed by many voters in Quebec as the third major rebuff of Quebec by the ROC within the past dozen years.

Indeed, the PQ's policy position for the moment is more reactive than proactive, counting on the ROC to patch together a package that offers less than the original Meech Lake agreement. PQ strategists also realize that a fair number of people in the ROC are convinced that the Quebec government is bluffing. Many people elsewhere in Canada also strongly believe that Quebec has no right to be treated differently from the other provinces. Indeed, the Reform party has gained substantial support in Western Canada on a platform calling for the equal treatment of provinces and the termination of official bilingualism. Furthermore, many Canadians believe that the nation is being hurt by Quebec's constant stream of demands, and some argue that Canada would be much better off in the long run, both politically and economically, without Quebec.

Thus, the emotional tide might swing in favor of the sovereignty option in Quebec if any of the following occur: (1) if the renewed federalism package is widely perceived in Quebec as falling far short of the guarantees offered to Quebec at Meech Lake; (2) if the renewed federalism package generally satisfies Bourassa's five conditions, but major groups in the ROC that feel betrayed by the constitutional agreement speak out bitterly against the proposed pact; (3) if the renewed federalism package satisfies the minimum conditions outlined at Meech Lake, but the national referendum leads to a rejection of the package by one or more provinces; (4) if resentment of Quebec's demands accelerate in the ROC, leading to demonstrations, the burning of Quebec's fleur-de-lys flag, growing support for political movements which are considered to be anti-Quebec, or other related activities; or (5) if, after an uncertain outcome in the national referendum, Robert Bourassa experiences a "road-to-Damascus" conversion and comes out in favor of the sovereignty option, claiming that over the long term, Quebec would be better off as an independent state.

Conversely, if the renewed federalism package is reasonable and is supported by the requisite number of provinces, if Bourassa can enthusiastically lead a referendum campaign in favor of renewed federalism instead of sovereignty, and if emotionalism generally takes a backseat to pragmatic arguments for or against the new constitutional package, then the odds are very good that Quebeckers will opt to remain an integral part of Canada for the foreseeable future.

If the national referendum results in significant support in both the ROC and Quebec for the renewed federalism package, will the sovereignty issue finally disappear? Not likely. The PQ, under new leadership after its referendum failure, may still form the next provincial government as a result of elections held in 1993. By that time, Bourassa will have served two consecutive terms and no provincial government has won a third consecutive mandate in decades. One must also realize that whether the Liberals or the PQ or some new third party forms a government in the future, all will continue to push for greater provincial control over most major sectors of Quebec society.[31] This is simply a "motherhood" issue for most Quebeckers and is unlikely to disappear from the political scene.

Furthermore, support for the notion that Francophone Quebeckers must ultimately protect their own language, culture, civil code, and way of life seems to be growing. Francophones may be a distinct minority in both Canada and North America, but they enjoy a huge majority within Quebec, and they already exercise control over tax collection, pension plans, the security force, job training, immigration, the legal system, language laws, and many other areas considered to be within the purview of a "sovereign" nation. Moreover, as Denis Monière argues, the decision on whether to be sovereign or not should be based on the future well-being of Francophone Quebeckers, rather than current concerns about pocketbook issues. He implores Quebeckers to recognize that independence is the best solution for safeguarding collective liberty, adding that "Quebec's independence will finally establish on this planet a territory and a political system reflecting our collective existence and guaranteeing our survival forevermore."[32]

Quebeckers will ultimately decide if their province will remain a part of Canada. Clearly, they now identify much more closely with Quebec than with Canada. Eventually, when economic conditions improve, they may be willing to absorb a drop in their living standards during a period of transition to independence. Time and numbers may also be on the side of the sovereigntists. The staunchest supporters of federalism in Quebec are Anglophones and older Francophones, both of which are diminishing groups. Conversely, the strongest supporters of sovereignty are younger, well-educated Francophones, and their ranks should swell over the next several years. Consequently, Quebeckers may eventually vote in favor of a referendum issue similar to the two-part question proposed by Pierre Bourgault: "(1) Do you want Quebec to become a sovereign country? (2) Do you want a sovereign Quebec, insofar as it is possible, to be associated economically with Canada?"[33]

Furthermore, if Quebec were to leave Canada with its current boundaries intact, it would rank as the seventeenth largest nation geographically and as the fifteenth largest in terms of GDP, equivalent to Sweden's and greater than the GDPs of Denmark, Norway, Austria, Greece, or Portugal. It would also rank as the ninth largest trading partner of the United States. With little doubt, this newly independent state would be politically and economically viable. However, if this state is ever established, it will be roundly criticized by the community of nations unless it extends broad civil, political, social, religious, and linguistic rights to its own minority groups. Consequently, if Quebec does opt for sovereignty at some juncture during the next quarter century, it should be expected to implement immediately a bill of rights with freedoms commensurate to those found in the United States and in Canada.

CHAPTER FIVE

ECONOMIC CHALLENGES FACING CANADA

E ven if Quebec and the ROC do work out their differences by the end of 1992, Canada will still face a formidable number of economic challenges. Canada's success in the economic arena is also important for the United States. Solid growth of gross domestic product in Canada should lead to greater exports for U.S. companies and to higher profits for U.S. affiliates situated north of the border.

In addition, Canada must play a key role if the North American marketplace envisioned in the FTA and the NAFTA is to compete effectively vis-à-vis the European Community and East Asia. In particular, U.S. corporations must be able to prosper in vibrant and growing markets to the north and south as a precursor to securing new business opportunities across the Atlantic and the Pacific. Conversely, stagnant markets north of the 49th parallel and south of the Rio Grande could represent a major setback for U.S. enterprises engaged in global commerce. To avoid such stagnation, Canada must find workable solutions to the following problems.

FEDERAL AND PROVINCIAL DEBT BURDENS

Proportionally, Canada's federal government debt burden is worse than that of the United States, although Ottawa has taken more substantive steps than Washington to contain its burgeoning debt, and Canada has a much higher savings rate to help finance this liability.[1] On the other hand, Washington has a much larger defense budget from which it can make cuts in the post–cold war era. Ottawa is currently spending $12.8 billion (C) on defense and plans to pare this budget by almost 20 percent over the next five years.[2] It devotes about 2 percent of GDP to defense and already ranks near the bottom of the NATO countries, with only Iceland and Luxembourg spending less as a percentage of GDP.[3] In contrast, the United States spends at least two and one-half times what Canada allocates for defense as a proportion of annual production.

At the end of the 1992–93 fiscal year, the Canadian federal government's cumulative debt will approach $450 billion (C), or about 65 percent of GDP versus 35 percent in 1980. Approximately 35 cents of every revenue dollar are used exclusively to pay interest on this debt. Unlike Washington, Ottawa has actually run an annual operating surplus over the past several years, but the $43 billion (C) in annual interest payments on the debt have still resulted in significant yearly deficits.[4]

Aggregate spending by provincial governments tops federal spending by about 15 percent per year. Unfortunately, all ten provincial governments are also in debt, and their fiscal situation is generally worse than the state governments south of the 49th parallel. Total provincial government deficits were in the range of $20 billion (C) for each of the 1991–92 and 1992–93 fiscal years, twice the level of the 1990–91 deficit. Aggregate provincial government debt at the end of fiscal year 1992–93 will be $165 billion (C). Moreover, the fiscal condition of the provinces will certainly not be helped by a cutback in federal transfer payments for the very expensive medicare program, from about 50 percent of costs to 35 percent.

The cumulative debt in Ontario at the end of the 1992–93 fiscal year will surpass $63 billion (C), of which over $20 billion (C) was added in just the past two years. Ontario is actually better off proportionally than several other provinces. Saskatchewan, for example, has had its debt rating reduced by Standard & Poor's to BBB+, a level that is considered as a "risky" investment by some funds specializing in government bonds. Saskatchewan's debt as a proportion of provincial production now surpasses 55 percent and is headed upward. Even the Alberta government, which has long prided itself on its fiscal acumen and which has been able to sock away billions of dollars of oil and gas royalties in its Heritage Fund, has run eight consecutive years of deficits and is now a net debtor province.[5]

Unless conditions change for the better, the cumulative debt for all levels of government in Canada will continue to grow substantially, and there is little indication that this debt is being used for infrastructure improvements, expanded research and development, or other activities that would make Canada more economically competitive in the years ahead. Already, public sector debt is equal to about 80 percent of GDP, and governments are spending about $55 to $60 billion (C) per year to service this debt. Lower interest rates will certainly drop the costs of borrowing by a substantial amount, but low interest rates must be combined with steady economic growth and more prudent spending habits if all levels of Canadian government are to surmount their debt difficulties.

EXTERNAL DEBTS

In absolute dollar terms, the United States and Canada rank as the two leading debtor countries in the world, owing more to foreign sources than any other developed or developing nation around the planet. Proportionally, however, Canada's external debt is much more serious than the U.S. debt burden.

The net indebtedness of Canada's public and private sectors to foreign sources is close to $270 billion (C).[6] Interest payments on this debt, combined with large international travel outlays, have resulted in six consecutive years of increases in Canada's current account deficit, with the record 1991 deficit of $27 billion (C) equaling almost 4 percent of GDP. In 1991, Canada actually ran a $3 billion (C) deficit with the United States in trade in goods and services, the first such deficit since 1977. Most of this borrowing in the United States and overseas financial markets is attributable to the federal and provincial governments and to their publicly owned corporations. Once again, lower interest rates, cutbacks in government borrowing, and an increase in exports will be needed before Canada can begin to reduce its large current account deficits.

DOMESTIC TRADE BARRIERS

Ottawa now has a free trade agreement with the United States, but it has not yet achieved economic union within Canada itself. An estimated five hundred provincial barriers currently impede the free flow of goods, services, capital, and labor within the confederation. The Canadian

Manufacturers' Association estimates that these barriers or subsidies cost Canadian consumers $5 billion (C) per year, or about 1 percent of annual GDP, adding that "it is easier to trade between Canada and the United States now with free trade than it is to trade between provinces."[7] These barriers also complicate the efforts of the business community to become more globally competitive.

The obstacles to interprovincial trade include licensing stipulations, "buy province" procurement provisions, transportation regulations, construction restrictions, and subsidies to local enterprises. As an illustration, Quebec's construction laws prevent workers elsewhere in Canada from being employed in the province.[8] These laws also mandate that during the last two weeks in July, construction must shut down, even though this is one of the best periods to work in a country known for long, harsh winters.[9] As another example, Americans have long been able to buy Moosehead Beer made in New Brunswick, but in an effort to protect local breweries, most provincial governments banned the sale of Moosehead to their consumers, a ban that the provinces finally agreed to end on July 1, 1992.[10] As a further illustration, a Nova Scotian traveling by bus to Quebec must change bus lines at the New Brunswick border, because the New Brunswick government forbids Nova Scotia bus companies from using its roads.[11]

Efforts are under way to reduce many of these barriers, with a 1995 deadline currently targeted. In separate negotiations, the four Western provinces and the three Maritime provinces are also attempting to erase regional impediments.[12] Furthermore, government procurement barriers began to be dismantled in April 1992. This multilateral agreement among the federal, provincial, and territorial governments applies to public tender offers for contracts covering the purchase of goods worth more than $25,000 (C). However, the agreement leaves much to be desired because it does not cover the procurement of services or contracts in the construction industry, nor does it apply to purchases made by schools, hospitals, municipal governments, or state-owned corporations.

To its credit, the Mulroney government has proposed that provisions be added to the constitution that will promote a national economic union. It is likely, however, that these provisions will be watered down and thus will have a minimal impact on domestic commerce.[13] Moreover, a constitutional provision agreed to by federal officials and the nine provincial premiers on July 7, 1992, but put on hold at Charlottetown, could have a devastating effect on the Canadian common market. Although giving lip service to the notion of economic union, this draft exempts thirteen different types of barriers and would actually list these exemptions within the new constitutional document. The decentralization thrust in other parts of the constitutional package would also accentuate economic balkanization within Canada.[14]

Canada needs the equivalent of the U.S. Interstate Commerce Commission or some other body that can resolve disputes across provincial boundaries. In addition, Section 121 in the Constitution Act, 1867 needs to be expanded to include more than the free movement of goods. Instead of greater decentralization in this sector, Ottawa and the provincial governments should join together to eliminate barriers and to harmonize standards, regulations, and administrative practices, thereby creating a much more effective national economic union.

QUESTION MARKS ABOUT COMPETITIVENESS

Some Canadians are now having second thoughts about the ability of their nation to compete economically within the North American market, let alone markets across the Atlantic and the Pacific. The Swiss-based World Economic Forum has also moved Canada down from fourth to fifth in its most recent ranking of the most competitive industrialized nations. More importantly, the Forum noted an increasing competitiveness gap between the higher-ranked United States and Canada, a conclusion echoed by the Economic Council of Canada.[15] The council found that production costs in Canada in 1991 were 40 percent higher than in the United States, whereas they were only 2 percent higher in 1980.[16] Judith Maxwell, the head of the Economic Council, provided the following explanation for the gap: "The problem is deeply rooted in Canadian society—we tend to resist change, we avoid competition and we try to shield ourselves from world economic forces."[17] In his costly report for the Canadian government and the Business Council on National Issues, Michael Porter echoed this criticism, chiding Canadian business managers and urging that they learn how to compete more effectively in nonresource sectors.[18] A Price-Waterhouse study added more salt to the wound, insisting that ambitious Canadians could increase their disposable income by at least 40 percent by emigrating to the United States.[19]

The recession in Canada during the 1990–92 period was much more profound than in the United States, ranking as Canada's worst since the

Great Depression. Approximately 450,000 jobs were lost in the period from April 1990 to April 1992, many in the manufacturing sector concentrated in central Canada. The unemployment rate stood at 11.6 percent in July 1992, the highest in eight years and the highest among the Group of Seven nations. More than 1.5 million Canadians were officially out of work, and some of Canada's largest corporations, including Edper and Olympia & York, have suffered major setbacks during the recession.

By the end of the 1980s, Canada's manufacturing productivity was about 70 percent of U.S. productivity.[20] Taxes are also appreciably higher in Canada, although they pay for a much more comprehensive health plan and overall safety net for all Canadian citizens.[21] In 1992, the average family income in Canada was estimated to be $53,535 (C). Taxes levied by all levels of government absorbed $23,537 (C) of that income, or 44 percent of total income.[22] During the most recent recession, higher taxes also absorbed over 60 percent of the meager income gains achieved by Canadians.[23] Gasoline prices are also about twice as high in Canada as in the United States, with the difference in price attributable to higher federal and provincial taxes. In the long run, this might be a farsighted policy if it promotes conservation and alternative transportation modes, but for the moment it contributes to the competitiveness gap with the United States.

Because most of Canada's citizens live within an hour's drive of the United States, they have opted to travel southward in record numbers and to purchase an estimated $5 billion per year of less expensive U.S. products and services. The sales tax burden is also more modest in the border states. Whereas the combined federal-provincial sales tax in Canada ranges from 7 percent in Alberta to almost 20 percent in Newfoundland, the sales tax in border states ranges from 0.0 percent in Montana and New Hampshire to 6.5 percent in Washington.[24]

The National Task Force on Cross-Border Shopping determined that Canada's distribution system is simply much less efficient than its U.S. counterpart. Canadian wholesalers are considerably smaller and this reduces their bargaining power with manufacturers. U.S.-made goods often pass through an additional level of distribution in Canada, thereby increasing the retail price. Moreover, manufacturers often charge Canadian distributors more than U.S. distributors because they perceive the cost of doing business in Canada to be greater and consider that the Canadian market is less strategically important to them. Furthermore, rents and leases, transportation costs, tariffs, and taxes are generally higher in Canada than in the United States.[25] The study also found that retail prices in Canada are higher because Canadian retailers, manufacturers, and distributors take steeper markups than their U.S. rivals.[26]

Unionization and union militancy are also more pronounced in Canada than the United States, although both countries have had relatively few disruptions in recent years.[27] About one-third of Canada's work force is unionized, almost double the rate of unionization in the United States.[28] Approximately 80 percent of those in Canada's public administration and over 70 percent in education are unionized, and it has been in Canada's huge public sector, which consists of employees in education, health care, welfare services, and the public administration, where militancy has been the most pronounced. This sector accounts for almost 24 percent of the total jobs in Canada, and employment in this sphere grew by 113,000 in 1991, a sharp contrast to the loss of 2.5 percent of jobs in the private sector.[29] In addition, wage settlements in many federal, provincial, and municipal public sectors have outpaced the rate of inflation during the recent recession. For the sake of competitiveness, government leaders must be willing to stand up to union militants and either limit increases in wages and fringe benefits or pare back the number of employees. The engine for future growth in Canada will be concentrated in the private sector, and policies must be implemented that will give this sector an opportunity to expand and to modernize.

CHAPTER SIX

POLITICAL AND SOCIAL
CHALLENGES FACING CANADA

anada must also confront a number of political and social challenges in its effort to become more competitive within North America and around the world. Problems such as falling graduation rates, escalating health and social welfare costs, adequate accommodation of new immigrant groups, and widespread disenchantment with political leadership are shared by both Canadians and Americans. On the other hand, the serious nature of the challenges linked to center-periphery inequities and the implementation of aboriginal self-government is distinctively Canadian and will require distinctive Canadian solutions.

HEARTLAND-HINTERLAND TENSIONS AND DISPARITIES

Political and economic power in Canada is basically centered in the Central Canadian provinces of Ontario, and to a lesser extent, Quebec. Although there are ten provinces and two territories in Canada, Ontario and Quebec account for over 62 percent of the population, 59 percent of the seats in the House of Commons, and 65 percent of the gross domestic product (see Table 1). By tradition, six of the nine Supreme Court judges come from these two provinces. The capital city, Ottawa, is also located in Ontario but is situated just across the river from Quebec. Indeed, several of the federal offices have been built in Ottawa's neighboring city, Hull, Quebec.

To place this within the context of the United States, California and New York, the two most populous states, have only 19 percent of total U.S. population, 19 percent of the seats in the House of Representatives, and 22 percent of the GDP. They are also separated by almost three thousand miles and there is no tradition of selecting a certain number of Supreme Court justices from either state. If one were to compare the so-called Boston–Washington, D.C. power corridor with Ontario and Quebec, the differences are still remarkable. In the area between Massachusetts and the District of Columbia, there are nine states and one federal district.[1] They account for 24 percent of the nation's population, 24 percent of the seats in the House of Representatives, and 27 percent of the GDP.

Table 1
Population, Area, and Gross Provincial Product of the Canadian Provinces and Territories

	Population (July 1991)	Area (km2)	Gross Provincial Product (1990) (C$ Billions)	Average Personal Income (C$)
Alberta	2,525,000	661,185	71.2	22,477
British Columbia	3,219,000	947,800	81.1	22,955
Manitoba	1,097,000	649,947	24.0	19,276
New Brunswick	727,000	73,437	13.2	17,778
Newfoundland	574,000	405,720	8.7	16,553
Nova Scotia	901,000	55,490	16.9	18,573
Ontario	9,919,000	1,068,582	281.2	25,386
Prince Edward Island	130,000	5,657	2.0	16.847
Quebec	6,851,000	1,540,680	157.2	20,988
Saskatchewan	997,000	652,330	20.4	17,941
Northwest Territories	54,800	3,426,320	(3.0*)	26,327
Yukon	27,000	483,450	(*combined)	25,815

Ontario by itself plays a much more dominant role in the Canadian confederation than either the California–New York or Massachusetts–D.C. combinations. It singlehandedly accounts for 36 percent of Canada's population, 34 percent of the seats in the House of Commons, and 41 percent of GDP. Half of Canada's manufacturing jobs are located within the boundaries of Ontario, and it continues to attract the bulk of new manufacturing facilities. During the 1980s, 54 percent of the growth of foreign direct investment in Canada occurred in Ontario. Toronto serves as not only the provincial capital, but also as the national headquarters for many of the major corporations, banks, and the media.

The utter domination of Ontario on the national landscape means that it would be very difficult for the ROC to survive as a nation if Quebec were to separate. An independent Quebec with its borders intact would divide the ROC in two, with five provinces to the west of Quebec and four to the east. In this new bifurcated nation, Ontario would have half the population and 54 percent of the GDP.[2] It would dominate politically and economically to a degree almost unprecedented within the advanced industrial world. Moreover, many parts of "Outer Canada" are already disenchanted with the dominant position of Central Canada, and would have serious reservations about placing their destiny in the hands of a smaller, bifurcated confederation dominated to an even greater degree by Ontario.

The term Western alienation is often bandied about in Canada and refers to the perception in the Western provinces, particularly in Alberta, that confederation has dealt them a bad hand. A fair number of people in the Canadian West believe that their region has been treated as a resource colony by Central Canada. They also complain that what is construed in Ottawa as "national policy" is actually "Central Canadian" policy. For example, they insist that the Bank of Canada initiated a tight money policy at the end of the 1980s in reaction to an overheated Ontario economy, at a time when much of the rest of the country was having difficulty in creating any new jobs at all.

This resentment is especially acute in Alberta, Canada's major oil and natural gas producer. The legacy of Pierre Trudeau as prime minister is very tarnished in Alberta and other parts of the West, and at one time his Liberal party failed to elect a single member to Parliament in the vast region between Winnipeg and the Pacific Ocean. For the sake of the "national interest," Trudeau's government mandated that the domestic price of oil in Canada would be kept far below the world price during the period when the OPEC cartel basically determined both the global supply and pricing of petroleum. By 1980, the domestic price had fallen to 40 percent of the world price. In frustration, Alberta Premier Peter Lougheed said he might exercise the province's constitutional right to control its natural resources and simply shut off the oil tap. In turn, Trudeau threatened to send in troops and seize the oil fields in order to safeguard the well-being of the nation. Robert Mansell, a University of Calgary economist, estimates that federal government policies related to oil and natural gas pricing cost the Alberta economy $66 billion (C) from the early 1970s through the mid-1980s, while at the same time benefiting the Ontario and Quebec economies by $42.5 and $14.4 billion (C) respectively.[3]

These tensions also help to explain the strong support for the Triple-E Senate in Alberta. After Trudeau and his Liberal party won reelection in February 1980, but without any seats west of Winnipeg, his National Energy Program (NEP) was ratified by a simple majority vote in the House of Commons and the Senate. The NEP kept the price of Alberta's oil and natural gas well below world levels. It also created a new federal export tax on natural gas so that Ottawa could reap some of the profits from the sale of Alberta gas, at global prices, to the United States (Ottawa already had a similar tax on exported oil). The NEP also created incentives for oil companies to explore and develop fields on federal lands in the north and offshore, helping to divert some development activity from Alberta. Moreover, impediments were placed on foreign companies involved in the oil and gas sector, prompting a stream of protests from Washington. Many of these mostly U.S.-owned enterprises were headquartered in Alberta.[4]

With the Triple-E Senate in place, Outer Canada would control more seats than Central Canada. The Senate would also have an equal voice vis-à-vis the House of Commons, at least in matters touching on the control and taxation of natural resources. Therefore, from Alberta's vantage point, the Triple-E Senate would make it much more difficult for any future government in Ottawa to implement NEP-style legislation.

Both Western and Atlantic Canada are also more heavily dependent on resource extraction than Central Canada and resent that they have not been able to attract manufacturing and other value-added industries that would help them mitigate the effects of "boom-or-bust" resource economies. On the other hand, the West, especially British Columbia and Alberta, are far better off economically than the four Atlantic provinces of New Brunswick, Nova Scotia, Prince Edward Island, and Newfoundland. All four provinces have average annual incomes well below the national average and are very dependent on financial support from Ottawa and "transfer payments" from the "have" provinces to the "have-nots."[5]

Newfoundland provides the extreme example of how poorly the wealth of Canadian society is distributed on a geographic basis. In an economic strategy paper released by the Newfoundland government headed by Clyde Wells, it was estimated that 29 percent of the gross income of Newfoundlanders was derived from unemployment insurance, social assistance, and other government transfer programs. At the end of 1991, eighty-five thousand residents of Newfoundland, out of a total work force of 238,000, collected unemployment insurance.[6] With the future of the $5 billion Hibernia offshore oil development project, the only large-scale job-creation scheme in all of Atlantic Canada, now in doubt, and the collapse of the northern cod fisheries, Newfoundland may face a much bleaker economic future than any other North American region, at a time when its unemployment rate already tops 20 percent.[7] The situation elsewhere in Atlantic Canada is somewhat better but is still quite ominous.

The current geographic distribution of Canada's population, wealth, industry, resources, and political and corporate power lends itself to regional tensions and mistrust. Canada's system of transfer payments from the richer provinces to the poorer provinces is much more enlightened than the U.S. system of grants-in-aid, but regional profiles are also much more skewed in Canada than in the United States. For example, on the remote North Atlantic island of Newfoundland, 580,000 people are scattered among eight hundred communities along ten thousand miles of coastline. Without a viable fishing industry, it is virtually impossible for many of these people to make a decent living. For the sake of fiscal sanity, Ottawa may have to consider cutting back on transfer payments, which help people subsist in areas such as Newfoundland where the outlook for job creation is miserable. Instead, incentives should perhaps be offered to those willing to relocate to regions where jobs are relatively plentiful. This flies in the face of a noble Canadian tradition of being able to live in the province where one was raised, but in an age when a nation hopes to remain globally competitive, labor mobility may be an essential ingredient for success.

ABORIGINAL CLAIMS

The current set of constitutional negotiations should result in aboriginal groups receiving greater recognition, authority, and benefits than at any time since the confederation was founded in 1867. Aboriginal government may become the third official level of government in Canada's federal system. Aboriginals may also be entitled to self-government, control over significant amounts of territory and resources, and financial support to help them establish governing institutions and procedures.

There may be anywhere from a half million to over one million aboriginals in Canada, divided into groups known as Status Indians, non-Status Indians, the Inuit, and Métis. Status Indians are similar to federally recognized Indians in the United States. They are registered under Canada's Indian Act and are accorded certain rights, including the right to live on a reserve. In contrast, non-Status Indians are not registered and generally do not have these special rights.

Many aboriginals live in poverty and are poorly educated. A report released by a House of Commons Special Committee in 1983 provided the following gloomy details about the plight of aboriginals: (1) they are only one-quarter as likely to finish school as others in Canada; (2) their children are five times more likely to end up in the care of the state; (3) they are ten times likelier to go to jail; (4) their suicide rate is three times higher; (5) their average income is one-half to two-thirds the national average; and (6) their newborns are 60 percent more likely to die within four weeks.[8]

With this in mind, aboriginals deserve an opportunity to govern themselves, and much of what has been agreed to during the constitutional deliberations should be applauded. Nevertheless, far more precision is needed before an agreement should be signed with the aboriginal groups. For example, how does one define who is an aboriginal and who is not? How might Métis' land claims differ from those of the Status Indians? How much territory will be turned over to the aboriginals? Should the people of each province be asked to approve, either through their provincial legislature or through a referendum, any land claims and other agreements reached by the federal and aboriginal governments? Will the self-governing areas be subject to Canada's Charter of Rights and Freedoms? For example, Canadian law and aboriginal law may differ in the treatment of women. Which law will prevail? If an aboriginal is accused of committing a crime against a nonaboriginal, or vice versa, which system of law will be used? How will aboriginal self-government be financed? What impact will this new level of government have on the movement of goods, services, labor, and capital within Canada?

Several years of negotiations will be needed before these and other questions can be sorted out. Moreover, decision-making power should not be abdicated to the federal court system. These issues are so important and so sweeping that only the elected representatives of Canadian aboriginals and nonaboriginals should make the final decisions, or the people should be consulted directly through the referendum process.

Canadians as a whole believe that aboriginal groups deserve more control over their own destinies. This goodwill undoubtedly will result in many gains being achieved by these groups. However, the process will take time and the final agreement must take into account what is good for the aboriginals, what is good for nonaboriginals, and what is good for Canada as a nation-state.

ADAPTATION TO MULTICULTURALISM

It is increasingly irrelevant within the Canadian context to speak of two founding peoples and the bilingual and bicultural nature of Canadian society. Aboriginals object to this portrayal, claiming with great justification that they constitute the "first nation"; and so do the millions of Canadians who descend neither from French nor English stock. In 1957, of the top ten nations supplying immigrants to Canada, nine were in Europe and the tenth was the United States. In 1974, three were European and one was the United States. In 1991, the top ten nations were, in order of importance in supplying immigrants, Hong Kong, Poland, China, India, the Philippines, Lebanon, Vietnam, the United Kingdom, El Salvador, and Sri Lanka.[9] Canada welcomed over 200,000 permanent immigrants in 1991 and is expected to open its borders to another 250,000 in 1992, triple the figure of just eight years ago and proportionally higher than the number who will enter the United States. Fewer and fewer of these immigrants have any attachments to Great Britain or to France.

From 1981 to 1986, net immigration accounted for 21 percent of Canada's total population growth. From 1986 to 1991, this figure jumped to 38 percent. What Canadians refer to as "visible minorities" (non-Caucasians and nonaboriginals) now constitute about 10 percent of Canada's population, and this should increase to about 18 percent by the turn of the century. At that time, 45 percent of the population of Toronto will be from this group, as will be about 40 percent of the population of Vancouver and from 20 to 25 percent of the populations of Montreal, Edmonton, Calgary, and Winnipeg.[10]

Multiculturalism is now clearly in evidence in Canada, and the clash of cultures and beliefs is causing frictions that Canadians have usually associated with the United States. Some old-time Canadians believe that traditional Canadian values are being eroded as more and more immigrants arrive on Canada's shores. Some were aghast that a federal court permitted a Sikh who had joined the Mounties to wear his traditional headdress instead of the standard Mountie hat. Many believe that immigrants should be wholeheartedly committed to learning English (or French in Quebec) and embracing the values enshrined in Canada's Constitution Acts and the Charter of Rights and Freedoms. Others, such as those who support the platform of the Reform party, believe that the federal government has no business promoting official multiculturalism.

Quite frankly, there is no such thing as English Canada, and the notion of French Canada is being increasingly blurred as a rainbow spectrum of immigrants enters both Quebec and the ROC. Tensions will undoubtedly increase in Canada's highly urbanized society as misperceptions and misunderstandings occur between the various ethnic and racial groups. Enlightened policies and attitudes will be needed to overcome prejudices and stereotyped images. If Canada is successful in doing so, and is able to provide a solid education and good skills for these new immigrants, it will become a far more competitive nation in the twenty-first century.

THE FRAGILE SAFETY NET

Canada introduced universally accessible medicare in 1971 and its health care system is far superior to that of the United States.[11] In addition, most Canadians continue to be either satisfied or very satisfied with the health care available to them.[12] Canada now spends 9 percent of its GDP on health care and covers all of its 27.5 million people. In contrast, the United States spends more than 12 percent but provides no coverage for thirty-five million Americans. Tens of millions of additional Americans are also considered to have inadequate health care insurance.

Nevertheless, Canada is currently spending $71 billion (C) per year on health care and its expenditures as a percentage of GDP are the second highest in the Western world. Even more worrisome, health care costs are climbing dramatically. Ottawa has cut back its contribution to provincially run medicare programs, and provinces are beginning to collect fees for various services or are eliminating coverage of certain procedures. The funding challenge is the greatest faced by Canada since the introduction of medicare, and the time-honored notion of universality is now being threatened.

Furthermore, Canada's poverty rate is now slightly higher than in 1980, and is expected to increase over the decade. Indeed, the Economic Council of Canada predicts that one-third of all Canadians will experience poverty over the course of their working lives. According to the Economic Council, family breakdown and the resulting growth in single-parent homes help to explain why an increase in the level of poverty is expected.[13] If this does occur later in the 1990s, provincial budgets will have to absorb greater social-welfare costs.

One must add, however, that being "poor" in Canada is a more comfortable existence than being poor in the United States. Canada's safety net is much more comprehensive, even for those who live in poverty. Moreover, Ottawa's definition of poverty is more liberal than Washington's. In 1961, Ottawa defined a family of three as living in poverty if its income was below $3,000 (C) (or $14,969 (C) in 1990 dollars). In 1990, a family of three living in a big city was considered to be poor if its income fell below $24,255 (C), whereas the latest federal poverty standards for a family of three in the United States was little more than half Canada's level. Canadians today are much wealthier than thirty years ago, and this generally includes low-income households as well.[14]

STRAINS IN THE EDUCATION SYSTEM

The high school dropout rate in Canada has now reached 30 percent, and the test scores of students have generally been on a downward slope over the past two decades. Close to 20 percent of Canadians are also considered to be functionally illiterate.[15] During the recent period of rising unemployment in Quebec, the Conseil du Patronat, which represents large firms employing 70 percent of Quebec's workers, complained that eighty thousand jobs were unfilled because of a lack of skilled personnel.[16] These problems in the educational arena have occurred in spite of Canada spending more per capita on education than any other Western nation except Sweden. In the area of worker training, however, Canadian companies spend per employee only one-half, one-fifth, and one-eighth of what U.S., Japanese, and German companies allocate, respectively.[17]

Although the U.S. dropout rate is somewhat lower than Canada's, the problems facing Canada in the educational arena are probably less severe. In international achievement tests in mathematics and the sciences, Canadian students usually do better than their American counterparts. Moreover, Canada has much tougher graduation standards and generally demands much more of the student in the classroom. However, in comparison with Japan's 4 percent dropout rate and very low functional illiteracy rate, tough education standards, and continuous training of the work force, Canada's system of education leaves much to be desired.

DISENCHANTMENT WITH POLITICAL LEADERSHIP

At this moment, it is an excruciating task to predict which parties and which individuals will lead the Canadian government later in the 1990s. Brian Mulroney hopes to settle the Quebec issue and see a marked recovery in the economy before he calls an election in 1993. At one time, more Canadians believed that Elvis Presley was still alive than believed Brian Mulroney was doing a good job as prime minister. Nevertheless, a widely applauded settlement of the unity and constitutional questions, combined with a robust economic recovery and the creation of tens of thousands of new jobs, could conceivably result in a victory for Mulroney or whoever leads the Progressive Conservative party into the next election. Most Canadians, however, now consider this to be a remote possibility.

On the other hand, if Quebec's voters were to reject the renewed federalism package and then support a referendum issue favoring sovereignty, Brian Mulroney and Liberal party leader Jean Chrétien, both native sons of Quebec, would most likely be looking for new jobs.

The political waters have been further muddied by the addition of two new regionally based parties since the last parliamentary elections were held in 1988. Polls indicate that the Reform party has from 12 to 15 percent support in provinces outside of Quebec, with its strongest following in Alberta. Its leader, Preston Manning, is Canada's closest equivalent to Ross Perot. The Reform party supports the Triple-E Senate and free trade with the United States. It rejects the notion of a distinct society status for Quebec and wants the federal government to abandon official bilingualism and official multiculturalism. It is expected to do well in Alberta and, depending on the outcome of the constitutional discussions and the outlook for the economy, could win additional seats from Ontario westward.

The Bloc Québécois (BQ) is directed by Lucian Bouchard, a former confidant of Mulroney who, after the failure of the Meech Lake accord, led a group of Quebec Conservative MPs across the neutral zone in the House of Commons to sit on the opposition benches. The BQ has a close working relationship with the PQ and is dedicated to taking Quebec out of Canada through democratic means. It currently enjoys significant support in Quebec and its fortunes depend on what type of settlement, if any, is reached between Quebec and the ROC in the current constitutional discussions.

At the provincial level, over 50 percent of Canada's population is now governed by a political party that has never formed a national government. The New Democratic Party (NDP) is the continent's largest and most devoted social-democratic movement, with the possible exception of Mexico's Party of the Democratic Revolution (PRD) led by Cuauhtemoc Cardenas. It is also the one major party in North America that has a woman, Audrey McLaughlin, as its leader. The NDP deeply opposes free trade with the United States and Mexico and supports more state intervention in the economic sector. Bob Rae, Roy Romanow, and Mike Harcourt currently lead NDP governments in Ontario, Saskatchewan, and British Columbia. Romanow and Harcourt have generally maintained cordial relations with their business communities and have opted for middle-of-the-road solutions to many economic problems. On the other hand, Rae and some of his cabinet colleagues got off to a rocky start with the Ontario business community and have been roundly blamed for Ontario's deep recession. Business leaders in Toronto remain very suspicious of the close ties between the NDP and organized labor and have frowned long and often because of NDP policies linked to deficit spending, workers' rights, pay equity, and other issues. A billboard at the corner of a busy intersection in downtown Toronto features a picture of Rae with the caption: "Buffalo Business Boosters' Man of the Year."[18] This is in reference to the number of Ontario businesses that have left the province and set up shop in the neighboring state of New York.

The Canadian public is not enthusiastic about any party or any political leader. When asked to select between Mulroney, Chrétien, McLaughlin, and Manning in terms of who would make a good prime minister, "none of the above" usually wins. The public is discouraged and somewhat embittered because of the lingering recession and the everlasting constitutional discussions. They do not believe that the government responds to their needs and told the commission led by Keith Spicer that they would be willing to experiment with an American-style system. Ironically, Americans increasingly feel that their own system of government responds far too much to special interests and not nearly enough to the aspirations of the rank-and-file citizen.

The Canadian voters are clearly unhappy with the current crop of political leaders and are not very enthusiastic about any political movement. Their votes in the next election will depend significantly on pocketbook issues and how they respond to the final constitutional package or the lack of such a package. This is a volatile period and major changes in political preference could be forthcoming. Moreover, if all five parties survive the constitutional juggernaut and are successful in electing members to the House of Commons, the Canadian Parliament may bear some resemblances to the Italian Parliament. Coalition building could be difficult, and a minority government might have to labor mightily just to pass the most menial of legislation. This type of gridlock and stalemate would simply add to the frustrations of the Canadian electorate.

CHAPTER SEVEN

CANADA-U.S. TRADE ISSUES IN PERSPECTIVE

No bilateral trading relationship is as deep or as diverse as that existing between the two nations that share a border at the 49th parallel. There is also an unusually close linkage between U.S. trade and investment activity with Canada, with nearly one-half of total U.S. exports to Canada, and more than one-third of Canadian exports to the United States, attributable to intracorporate transactions between U.S. parent firms and their majority-owned Canadian affiliates.[1]

In view of the expansive nature of the economic linkages, it should be expected that occasional disputes will arise. Indeed, a number of disagreements have arisen just in the period since the Canada-U.S. Free Trade Agreement began to be implemented in January 1989. These disputes cover the spectrum from softwood lumber to fruit, pork, cars, beef, beer, wine, minerals, natural gas, carpet, gypsum wallboard, plywood, paving equipment, steel, and so on. Some of these disputes, especially softwood lumber, are vital both to national and regional economies. Most, however, represent a very tiny sliver of a very big pie, and generally trade is occurring with a minimum of friction. Consequently, as headlines are being written, especially in Canada, about the numerous frictions that exist between Ottawa and Washington, the cross-border trade, investment, and tourism linkages continue quietly to expand and to provide new jobs for residents on both sides of the 49th parallel. Moreover, because of the nature of the coverage of the issue, few Canadians and Americans are aware that various industries in their countries have mutually agreed to accelerate the FTA timetable for the elimination of tariffs.

CANADIAN AMBIVALENCE TOWARD FREE TRADE WITH THE UNITED STATES

On paper, the FTA has been a success for Canada. In spite of the recession, Canadian exports to the United States have grown significantly since 1989, although they tailed off slightly during the deepest part of the recession in 1991. Exports have once again rebounded in 1992, with the highest level of Canadian exports ever dispatched to the United States recorded in March. Canada has also been the net recipient of direct investment for the first time in many years, prompted in part by its improved access to the huge U.S. market.

Canadians should be warming up to the FTA, but most continue to be disenchanted with the accord and the proposed NAFTA.[2] A good part of this opposition is attributable to the fact that the FTA and the recession arrived at just about the same time. But the issue is more complicated than simply poor timing in implementing the FTA. The United States has inherited the role, by default, of being the world's only superpower when measured in strategic and military terms. In comparison with Canada, it is also almost ten times larger in population and economically. Canadians frequently worry about the elephant–mouse syndrome. As the story goes, when these two animals share the same bed, the mouse must always be vigilant, regardless of how well intentioned the elephant may be.

Two proponents of Canadian economic nationalism assert that "Canada is the most economically occupied country in the industrial world; no other country even comes close."[3] In many respects, this is a true statement. Canada has far more foreign ownership proportionally than any other Group of Seven country, and a majority of this ownership is American. Of the largest 500 corporations in Canada, 181 are foreign owned, with 104 of the 181 U.S.-controlled.[4] Especially outside of Quebec, most of the programs Canadians watch on television, or the magazines they read, or the movies they see at the local cinema are American-made.[5] Canada's cable systems carry not only local channels, but also ABC, CBS, NBC, PBS, and a host of other channels that emanate from the United States.

Quite frankly, many Canadians worry about being absorbed economically, culturally, or even physically by the United States. They are concerned that too many corporate decisions in Canada are made in New York City or Chicago rather than Toronto or Montreal. Some may also suffer from an inferiority complex, perceiving that true success in North America, whether they like it or not, means making it big in the United States. For example, some measure the achievements of Canadian performers by how well they do in Hollywood, on Broadway, or at Lincoln Center. A truly first rate graduate education is perceived as being offered by an Ivy League school instead of the University of Toronto or McGill University. Furthermore, in historical perspective, Canada has often served as a stepping-stone for immigrants whose ultimate goal may have been to enter the United States. Between 1860 and 1950, approximately 8.8 million people immigrated to Canada, but 6.8 million emigrated during the same period, mostly to the United States.

Canadian apprehensions permeate their attitudes toward the United States and Americans in general. In an extensive *Maclean's*-sponsored poll released in July 1989, Canadians were asked this question: "If you had to describe Americans in one word, what would it be?" The top ten responses were snobs, good, friendly, pigheaded, aggressive, powerful, obnoxious, indifferent, stupid, and rich. When Americans were asked the exact same question about Canadians, their top ten responses were friendly, nice, neighbors, wonderful, similar, satisfied, normal, delightful, northerners, and French.[6]

In part as a reflection of reality and in part as a defense mechanism, Canadians generally consider Americans to be more arrogant, chauvinist, violent, racist, materialist, individualist, and uncaring than they are. Diane Francis, editor of the *Financial Post*, moved from the United States to Canada more than two decades ago. Her reaction to the 1992 riots in Los Angeles would be echoed by many Canadians:

> Is there a Canadian who doesn't appreciate living here after witnessing the violence of social injustice south of the border? We think we have problems getting along with one another. Just try to imagine what it must be like to be black in a U.S. ghetto with rats, filth, families exposed to drugs, lousy schools, no medical attention and dangerous neighborhoods thanks to vicious gangs! Meanwhile, we're up here fighting fiercely over

whether the department of tourism should be run by Quebec or Ottawa.[7]

Canadians may like to shop and vacation in the United States, but they do not want to see their nation absorbed by their huge southern neighbor. Their sense of apprehension is more acute today than it has been for many years because the Quebec issue is eroding Canadian political unity at the same time that the FTA is strengthening continental economic integration. In a Gallup poll released in December 1991, 37 percent of Canadians thought their country would eventually be absorbed by the United States, up from 24 percent three years earlier.[8]

AN END TO THE FTA?

With this in mind, U.S. business leaders must recognize that there is a slight chance that the FTA may be altered or even abrogated within the next three years. A national government led by the NDP would be the most likely to demand major changes in the accord or to begin the six-month process of termination. An informal coalition between the Liberals and the NDP might also demand changes that Washington would be unwilling to accommodate.

The siren song of Fortress Canada would be an unmitigated disaster for the Canadian people. Of course, it is true that foreign investment in the Canadian economy is widespread, but its percentage of total assets in Canada has declined significantly over the past twenty years, from 37 percent of nonfinancial assets to 25 percent.[9] Moreover, the U.S. share of foreign direct investment in Canada declined during the 1980s.

Growing U.S. protectionism in the absence of the FTA would affect Canada more adversely than any other nation on earth. With 80 percent of its exports in recent months going exclusively to the U.S. market, and with export activity accounting for such a high proportion of GDP, Canada's economy could suffer dramatic reversals.

The United States is also the only major market with which Canada consistently enjoys a substantial merchandise trade surplus. Moreover, under the FTA, Canada has access to a dispute-settlement mechanism that is unavailable to all other U.S. trading partners. When a binational panel makes a ruling on an appeal of subsidy and dumping determinations, its decision is binding. Five judges sit on the panel, two from the United States, two from Canada, and one selected by mutual agreement of the first four judges. The panel rules on whether the laws of the nation have been faithfully followed. Canada has done very well in several recent cases, and some of the decisions have been by a vote of 5 to 0, meaning that national origin has not swayed the panelists.[10]

Both Canada and the United States must recognize that they are major players in an increasingly complex and interdependent international economy. Global trade in goods and services surpassed $4 trillion in 1991, at least a thirteenfold increase in real terms since 1950. The flow of international direct investment has increased even more rapidly, up tenfold in real terms from the end of the 1970s to the end of the 1980s. Between 1983 and 1989, international direct investment increased by an average of 29 percent per year, three times faster than the growth of exports and four times faster than the growth in world output.[11] No nation is capable of cutting itself off from this globalization trend without jeopardizing the standard of living and economic well-being of most of its citizenry.

For both countries, the FTA and the proposed NAFTA are critical accords that will strengthen the North American economy and prepare the business community to compete more effectively on a global scale. Without any doubt, Canada must endeavor to diversify its export markets, but through an expansion of its overall export activity rather than through a disastrous diminution in its trade flows with the United States. The formidable task facing Canada today is to forge a renewed sense of nationhood while resisting the shortsighted and utterly destructive policies being proffered by its economic nationalists.

CHAPTER EIGHT

THE CANADIAN
ECONOMY 2001

I n addition to the major political and social challenges it faces,
Canada will have to deal with: (1) the lowest levels of investment
in machinery, equipment, R & D, and training among the Group of
Seven nations;[1] (2) very high real interest rates, especially in comparison with U.S. rates; (3) projected low economic growth over the next
eighteen months;[2] (4) the continued toleration of interprovincial barriers and of marketing boards perpetuating supply-management policies;[3]
and (5) a very high unemployment rate topping 11 percent nationally
and over 20 percent in Newfoundland. If Canada were to apply for membership in the European Community and were asked to satisfy the five
"convergence" criteria for economic and monetary union, namely low
inflation rates, low long-term interest rates, low budgetary deficits, low
government debt, and low fluctuations in the value of its currency, it would
flunk three of the five tests.[4]

The Office of the U.S. Trade Representative (USTR) also devotes four-
teen pages in its annual *Foreign Trade Barriers* report to alleged unfair practices in Canada, second only to the eighteen pages devoted to Japan.
Washington's hit list includes provincial liquor boards, Canadian Wheat
Board licensing requirements, dairy, horticultural, and poultry import restrictions, plywood standards, the accreditation of U.S. firms, government

procurement codes, export subsidies, duty remission schemes, the lack of intellectual property protection, curbs on border broadcasting and U.S. advertising, discriminatory postal rates, investment barriers, and the imposition of performance requirements.[5]

On the other hand, Canada could actually emerge as one of the top-performing economies in the industrialized world within the next two or three years, providing excellent trade and investment opportunities for U.S.-based companies and investors. In fact, this is a plausible scenario if the following conditions are fulfilled:

• Quebeckers must react positively to the renewed federalism package presented by the ROC and the issue of Quebec sovereignty fades to the background for at least the next five to ten years.
• The new constitutional agreement cannot lead to a major erosion in Ottawa's authority and to an unacceptable level of decentralization.
• The new constitutional package cannot place major new financial burdens on Ottawa but can enhance Canada's economic union.
• Canada must retain the FTA with the United States.
• Canada must join the NAFTA (presuming it is finally ratified by the U.S. Congress).
• The federal and provincial governments must make a serious effort to reduce deficit spending and improve their fiscal situation.

Canadian exports are once again near record levels, and with the Canadian dollar falling in value by over 6 percent against the U.S. dollar between November 1991 and July 1992, prospects for continued growth in the export arena are very promising. Inflation is now well under control, falling to a thirty-year low during the first quarter of 1992. Interest rates have also dropped to levels not seen for more than two decades and are well below the Bank of Canada's target of 2 percent by the end of 1995. Real interest rates can be lowered further, and this will be of great benefit to most sectors of the economy and to debt-laden governments, corporations, and households. Indeed, every 1 percent drop in the bank rate saves Ottawa about $1.8 billion (C) a year in interest costs on the national debt.[6] The economic recovery might be slow at first but should pick up momentum as the U.S. economy also begins to grow. Labor productivity also improved markedly through the first half of 1992, and Canadian unit labor costs in manufacturing are now falling in relationship to U.S. costs. Beginning June 1, 1992, Ottawa also began to deregulate many of the activities of banks, trusts, and insurance companies, representing one of the most comprehensive reform plans in Canadian financial history. This deregulation should also improve prospects for enhanced business growth.[7]

With the special advantages offered by the FTA and proposed NAFTA, small and medium-sized U.S. businesses should be looking for good opportunities north of the border. In particular, they should cast aside the stereotyped image of Quebec as an inward-looking province that speaks a foreign language and is far too parochial. Just the opposite may be true. Some of the strongest support for an integrated North American market is centered in Quebec. Many of its business leaders are young and dynamic and are well versed in the challenges and opportunities to be found in a globalized economy.

A national agreement solidifying Canadian unity would also make other provinces attractive investment locations, with a provincial base permitting U.S. firms to service both the Canadian domestic market and overseas markets. The recent drop in the value of the Canadian dollar against the U.S. and other major currencies enhances Canada's position as a base for export activity. In addition, most provincial governments spend more money and are more actively involved in international trade and investment promotion than the U.S. state governments. Consequently, some U.S.-owned subsidiaries should be able to use the combination of a weaker Canadian dollar and provincial government export assistance to enhance their entry into third-country markets.

In conclusion, Canadians are going through one of the most difficult periods in their history, both politically and economically. If Quebec were to separate, both it and the ROC would suffer economic downturns in the short term, with Quebec's decline being more severe. Even if Quebec remains within Canada, a new constitutional arrangement that panders to the many clamoring interest groups could be devastating for the Canadian economy. On the other hand, Ottawa and the provincial governments can afford, in a revised package, to offer Quebec the five minimum conditions first put forward at Meech Lake. They can also put in motion aboriginal self-government and act to reform the anachronistic Senate, which has more in common with the British House of Lords than with any modern, democratically inspired parliamentary chamber. Conversely, these governments cannot afford across-the-board decentralization of powers. Moreover, they must vigorously push for the establishment of a true economic common market within Canada itself, and must recognize the growing importance of the FTA and eventually the NAFTA for the well-being of the people whom they represent.

Not only is Canadian nationhood at stake but also the ability of its business community to compete effectively continentally and globally. Rash moves over the next few months could easily jeopardize the standard of living of the Canadian people and could eventually lead to the division of Canada into two or more parts. Furthermore, a failure to maintain political and economic unity or a repudiation of regional trade agreements would make Canada a far less attractive trading and investment partner for the United States.

Statesmen and stateswomen should step forward and make enlightened decisions. Canada remains one of the most respected nations in the world, and though it is sparsely populated, its people have worked hard and pragmatically to develop the seventh largest economy and one of the highest standards of living on the planet. Canada has also been exemplary in its commitment to democratic values and in its leadership in pursuing peacekeeping opportunities globally. One of the great tragedies of the twentieth century would be for such a great nation to self-destruct.

NOTES

CHAPTER ONE

1. A remark made by an American journalist to Canadian Broadcasting Corporation reporter David Halton, CBC News Special, *Correspondents' Forum 1992*, May 5, 1992.

2. Episode of "Murphy Brown" aired May 4, 1992.

3. *Globe and Mail*, April 24, 1992, p. 48.

4. *Gallup Poll Monthly*, April 1991, pp. 29–30.

5. These data are for 1986 and are found in Harry H. Hiller, *Canadian Society: A Macro Analysis*, 2nd ed. (Scarborough, Ont.: Prentice Hall Canada, 1991), p. 51.

6. *Survey of Current Business*, May 1992, p. 61.

7. *Wall Street Journal*, February 18, 1992, p. A18, and Statistics Canada data.

8. Americans stayed an estimated 54 million nights in Canada in 1991 and spent $3.7 billion (C). See *Financial Times*, April 20, 1992, p. 11.

9. In 1988, for example, 92 percent of the international visits to Canada were made by residents of the United States. See Hiller, *Canadian Society*, p. 263.

CHAPTER TWO

1. See the comments of Allan Taylor in the *Toronto Star*, May 29, 1992, p. A13.

CHAPTER THREE

1. Harry H. Hiller, *Canadian Society: A Macro Analysis*, 2nd ed. (Scarborough, Ont.: Prentice Hall Canada, 1991), p. 11.

2. *Globe and Mail*, April 17, 1992, p. A1.

3. Keith Spicer, "Canada Needs a New Strategy of Hope," *Globe and Mail*, Forum Section, June 29, 1991, p. 1.

4. Allan R. Taylor, "The March of Folly," address to the shareholders of the Royal Bank, January 23, 1992.

5. *Maclean's*, June 8, 1992, p. 52.

CHAPTER FOUR

1. *Globe and Mail*, April 18, 1992, p. D1.

2. *Ottawa Citizen*, May 31, 1992, p. A4.

3. Jonathan Lemco, "Turmoil in the Peaceable Kingdom: The Quebec Sovereignty Movement and Its Implications for Canada and the United States," *Canada-U.S. Outlook*, nos. 1, 2, March 1992, p. 24.

4. Reed Scowen, *A Different Vision: The English in Quebec in the 1990s* (Don Mills, Ont.: Maxwell Macmillan Canada, 1991), p. 146. Many statistics on Anglophone-Francophone participation in the business sector are found in the Quebec Government's *Report of the Commission of Inquiry on the Position of the French Language and on Language Rights in Quebec* (Quebec: Éditeur Officiel du Québec, 1972), popularly known as the Gendron Commission. In 1971, the Anglophone-Francophone earnings gap was 33 percent, in 1980, 14 percent, and in 1992 it is anticipated that the gap may have disappeared.

5. Lemco, "Turmoil in the Peaceable Kingdom," p. 5.

6. *Financial Times*, May 4, 1992, pp. 1, 4.

7. The percentage of Quebeckers working in businesses controlled by Francophones rose from 55 percent in 1978 to 62 percent in 1987. See Brian Mulroney, "Canada's Future," speech to the Canadian and Empire Clubs, Toronto, February 12, 1991.

8. Quebec represented 36 percent of Canada's population in 1851, fifteen years before the establishment of the confederation, 30 percent in 1951, and about 25 percent in 1991.

9. Approximately nine out of ten Canadians whose only mother tongue is French now live in Quebec.

10. Neighboring New Brunswick is 31 percent Francophone. Between 1981 and 1986, the number of people in the ROC who spoke French at home decreased

from 3.8 percent to 3.6 percent. The Official Languages Act mandates that French will have equal standing with English in all services offered by the federal government. All consumer goods must also be labeled in both official languages.

11. *Globe and Mail*, April 13, 1992, pp. A1, A4.

12. Quebec will also receive from Ottawa $332 million (C) during the 1991–95 period to take over these new immigration responsibilities. In return, Ottawa retains the ultimate right to reject or to admit applicants, to control the arrival of refugees and sponsored immigrants, and to set national standards and objectives for immigration. See Lemco, "Turmoil in the Peaceable Kingdom," pp. 27–28.

13. *L'Actualité*, May 15, 1992, p. 11.

14. A recent poll found that only 5 percent of immigrants in Quebec supported the sovereignty option. See the *Globe and Mail*, June 19, 1992, p. A3.

15. *Globe and Mail*, February 3, 1992, p. A18.

16. *Ottawa Citizen*, May 25, 1992, p. A3.

17. Ibid.

18. Mordecai Richler, *Oh Canada! Oh Quebec!* (Toronto: Viking Penguin, 1992), p. 77 and Chapter 10.

19. Ibid., p. 107.

20. *Maclean's*, April 13, 1992, p. 28.

21. Pierre Bourgault, *Now or Never! Manifesto for an Independent Quebec* (Toronto: Key Porter, 1991), p. 116.

22. McGill University law professor Stephen A. Scott insists that a sovereign Quebec should not be allowed to keep the territory ceded to it in 1898 and 1912. See his article, "Secession or Reform? Mechanism and Directions of Constitutional Change in Canada," in *Federalism in Peril*, ed. A. R. Riggs and Tom Velk (Vancouver: Fraser Institute, 1992), pp. 149–162. Also consult Scott Reid, *Canada Remapped: How the Partition of Quebec Will Reshape the Nation* (Vancouver: Arsenal Pulp Press, 1992).

23. See, for example, Bourgault, *Now or Never!*, pp. 112–115.

24. *Gazette*, June 1, 1991, p. D5. The author has spoken directly to other members of the Canadian and U.S. negotiating teams and they generally insist that although Washington was unhappy with some Quebec policies, it did not single out Quebec quite to the extent emphasized by Reisman.

25. *Globe and Mail*, April 14, 1992, p. A17. One must keep in mind Canada's definition of poverty. In urban areas, in particular, the income threshold is much higher in Canada than in the United States. In other words, many people considered to be above the poverty line in the United States would be deemed by the Canadian government to be living in poverty.

26. Pierre Duhamel, "La faillite Doré," *Affaires Plus*, April 1992, pp. 28–30.

27. The brain drain is already under way. An inquiry by a Quebec newspaper in 1991 found that the top English-speaking graduates from Quebec's schools were unlikely to stay in the province because of better economic opportunities in other parts of Canada or in the United States. An account of this inquiry was featured in the *Ottawa Citizen*, May 25, 1992, p. A3.

28. *L'Actualité*, March 15, 1992, p. 26, and the *Gazette*, April 1, 1992, p. B3.

29. Norman Henchey and Donald Burgess, *Between Past and Future: Quebec Education in Transition* (Calgary: Detselig Enterprises, 1987), p. 200.

30. *Financial Post*, May 21, 1992, p. 3.

31. As Pierre Fournier points out, "to the extent that Quebeckers continue to identify with Quebec first, there will always be constitutional strife in Canada." He adds that the "affirmation nationale" will continue to develop and that it is tantamount to a motherhood issue for the political parties. See the *Ottawa Citizen*, May 23, 1992, p. A1.

McGill University sociologist Maurice Pinard has conducted a study showing that the number of Francophones who identify themselves as "Québécois" has risen from 21 percent in 1970 to 59 percent in 1990, whereas the number identifying themselves as Canadian has dropped from 34 percent to 9 percent during the same period. With both a growing emotional attachment to Quebec and emotional disengagement from Canada among Francophones, Pinard concludes, "I'm very pessimistic about keeping the country together." See ibid., p. A2.

32. Denis Monière, *L'indépendance* (Montreal: Québec/Amérique, 1992), p. 148. Translated into English by the author.

33. Bourgault, *Now or Never!* p. 129.

CHAPTER FIVE

1. Over the past twenty years, the net national savings rate in Canada has been 11 percent, compared with 6 percent in the United States and 23 percent in Japan. See Investment Canada, *Investing in Canada*, Summer 1992, p. 2.

2. One critic of these defense cutbacks, Joseph T. Jockel, insists that the Canadian armed forces are already "undermanned, underfunded, and underequipped." See his article, "Canada in the Post–Cold War World," *Current History*, December 1991, p. 407.

3. In spite of its meager spending on defense, Canada had more troops involved in international peacekeeping in 1990 than did any other country. In the post–cold war era, peacekeeping has assumed an added importance

(Yugoslavia, Cambodia, etc.), and no nation has had more experience in this area over the past 35 years than Canada.

4. The federal government's deficit was about $32 billion (C) in fiscal year 1991–92, and the target is $27.5 billion (C) for fiscal year 1992–93. Interest payments almost doubled just between 1984 and 1985 and 1991 and 1992.

5. *Globe and Mail*, April 13, 1992, p. B3.

6. This figure was compiled by Statistics Canada. See the *Globe and Mail*, April 3, 1992, p. B2.

7. *Financial Post*, April 17, 1991, p. 6.

8. *Globe and Mail*, June 17, 1992, p. A20.

9. *Financial Post*, May 25, 1992, p. S4.

10. The restrictions on interprovincial beer sales and on the pricing and availability of foreign-made beers and spirits are being relaxed or terminated, spurred on by complaints from GATT, Washington, and Canadian consumers. Provincial beer barriers actually date from 1928 when Ottawa handed the provinces jurisdiction over alcohol. See *Financial Post*, February 13, 1992, pp. 1 & 5.

11. *Los Angeles Times*, February 3, 1992, pp. A1 & A8.

12. The four provinces of New Brunswick, Nova Scotia, Prince Edward Island, and Newfoundland are collectively referred to as the Atlantic provinces. The first three are collectively referred to as the Maritime provinces.

13. Finance Minister Michael Wilson has pledged to work toward the elimination of interprovincial barriers by 1995, but has candidly admitted that he is facing stiff opposition from some provincial governments. See the *Globe and Mail*, June 5, 1992, p. B3.

14. See, for example, the arguments put forward in Richard G. Harris and Douglas D. Purvis, "Constitutional Change and Canada's Economic Prospects," *Canadian Public Policy* 17 (December 1991), pp. 379–394.

15. The information was contained in the Forum's 1991 World Competitiveness Report ranking twenty-four industrialized nations. See *Maclean's*, October 28, 1991, p. 37.

16. In the period 1985–90, Canadian unit labor costs in manufacturing increased by over 40 percent vis-à-vis the United States. Only two-fifths of this increase was attributable to the appreciation in the Canadian dollar.

17. *Financial Post*, February 13, 1992, p. 3.

18. Michael E. Porter, *Canada at the Crossroads: The Reality of a New Competitive Environment* (Ottawa: Business Council on National Issues and the Government of Canada, 1991).

19. *Maclean's*, October 28, 1991, p. 37.

20. In 1990 and 1991, manufacturing wages also crept up in Canada in comparison to the United States. In 1989, average hourly earnings in Canada were $13.54 (C) versus $12.41 (C) in the United States. In April 1991, the wages had increased to $15.04 (C) in Canada and $12.80 (C) in the United States. See the *Globe and Mail*, November 6, 1991, p. B23.

21. As a counterweight to higher taxes, fringe benefit packages offered by Canadian corporations are much less costly than comparable U.S. corporate packages.

22. These statistics were compiled by the Fraser Institute. The average Canadian family now works until June 10 to pay off its yearly tax obligations. See the *Financial Post*, June 29, 1992, p. 14.

23. From the first quarter of 1990 through the first quarter of 1992, higher taxes absorbed 61.5 percent of the increase in income. See the *Globe and Mail*, July 6, 1992, p. B1.

24. *Globe and Mail*, May 14, 1992, p. A18.

25. *Globe and Mail*, May 15, 1992, p. B6.

26. *Financial Post*, May 15, 1992, p. 9.

27. In 1991, the aggregate strike days in Canada tied 1985 for the lowest level in a quarter of a century. See the *Financial Post*, February 13, 1992, p. 6.

28. In 1989, only 19 percent of the industrial work force was unionized in Canada, but this is still well above comparable U.S. figures. See the *Financial Post*, May 28. 1992, p. 11.

29. *Globe and Mail*, February 21, 1992, p. A1.

CHAPTER SIX

1. Massachusetts, Rhode Island, Connecticut, New York, Delaware, Pennsylvania, New Jersey, Maryland, Virginia, and the District of Columbia.

2. *Globe and Mail*, January 20, 1992, pp. B1, B4.

3. *Alberta Report*, April 13, 1992, p. 17. Mansell's figures are expressed in 1990 Canadian dollars.

4. *Globe and Mail*, May 30, 1992, p. D6.

5. In 1991, only Ontario, Alberta, and British Columbia qualified as "have" provinces, meaning that some of the revenues that they paid to Ottawa were redistributed to the seven "have-nots." Total transfer payments from the donors are also quite substantial, representing around 3 percent of Ontario's GDP and over 8 percent of Alberta's GDP during the period 1980–88. Ontario's $10 billion (C) provincial deficit in the 1990–91 period was about the same as its contribution to Atlantic Canada. Premier Bob Rae has complained that Ontario

is the source for 43 percent of federal revenues but receives only 30 percent of federal expenditures. A good share of this revenue gap is attributable to the transfer payments. See Norman Cameron et al., *From East and West: Regional Views on Reconfederation* (Toronto: C.D. Howe Institute, 1991), pp. 104–5, 108; and *Maclean's*, June 8, 1992, p. 22.

6. *Globe and Mail*, June 19, 1992, p. A6.

7. In June 1992, Ottawa announced a two-year moratorium on cod fishing off the coast of Newfoundland, an action which may cost twenty thousand jobs. For a discussion of the cod issue, see Sharon Fraser, "When All the Fish Were Gone," *Canadian Forum*, May 1992, pp. 14–17. She blames this crisis on overfishing and on poor management of the fishing industry in general.

8. *Western Report*, January 13, 1992, p. 11.

9. *Globe and Mail*, June 20, 1992, p. A4.

10. These calculations are made by T. John Samuel, a research professor at Carleton University. See the *Gazette*, May 30, 1992, p. A1.

11. In 1971, Canada and the United States spent about the same percentage of GDP on health care. See the *New York Times*, November 21, 1991, p. A26.

12. In a *Globe and Mail* and CBC poll, 86 percent of Canadians stated that they were very satisfied or somewhat satisfied with the medical and hospital services which they receive. See the *Globe and Mail*, November 5, 1991, p. A6.

13. This report by the Economic Council of Canada was released in June 1992. See the *Globe and Mail*, June 26, 1992, p. A1.

14. *Globe and Mail*, January 13, 1992, p. A12.

15. *Financial Post*, May 5, 1992, p. 10.

16. *Alberta Report*, May 4, 1992, p. 6. It is estimated that several hundred thousand jobs are now available in Canada for those with adequate education and skills. See the *Financial Post*, May 5, 1992, p. 10.

17. Michael H. Wilson, "Planning Action to Avoid Economic Catastrophe," *Canadian Speeches*, December 1991, p. 13.

18. *Financial Times*, April 6, 1992, p. 13.

CHAPTER SEVEN

1. Investment Canada, "The Opportunities and Challenges of North American Free Trade: A Canadian Perspective," in *Investment in the North American Free Trade Area: Opportunities and Challenges*, ed. Earl H. Fry and Lee H. Radebaugh (Provo, UT: Brigham Young University David M. Kennedy Center, 1992), p. 165.

2. An Angus Reid Southam poll released in April 1992 indicated that two-thirds of Canadians were opposed to the FTA, versus 57 percent in a similar

poll conducted in 1990. In a *Financial Post*-COMPAS survey released in June 1992, 61 percent stated that the FTA was "damaging" to the interests of Canada, and 55 percent perceived that the NAFTA would place Canada at a further disadvantage. See the *Financial Post*, April 15, 1992, p. 11, and June 22, 1992, p. 3.

3. Maude Barlow and Bruce Campbell, *Take Back the Nation* (Toronto: Key Porter, 1991), p. 9.

4. *Financial Post 500*, 1992, pp. 92–125.

5. Harry H. Hiller, *Canadian Society: A Macro Analysis*, 2nd ed. (Scarborough, Ont.: Prentice Hall Canada, 1991), p. 263.

6. *Maclean's*, July 3, 1989, p. 49.

7. *Financial Post*, May 25, 1992, p. 51.

8. *Los Angeles Times*, February 3, 1992, p. A10.

9. Stuart A. Duncan, *Investment Performance in Canada: Understanding the Big Picture* (Calgary: Canada West Foundation, 1992), p. 7. The sectors with the highest percentage of foreign assets are manufacturing (46 percent), oil and gas (41 percent), and mining (31 percent).

10. For a review of some of the decisions rendered by the binational panels, consult Thomas M. Boddez and Alan M. Rugman, "Effective Dispute Settlement: A Case Study of the Initial Panel Decisions under Chapter Nineteen of the Canada-U.S. Free Trade Agreement," and Harry B. Endsley, "Dispute Settlement under the Canada-U.S. Free Trade Agreement: Review and Assessment," in Fry and Radebaugh, eds., *Investment in the North American Free Trade Area*, pp. 93–126 and 127–154.

11. *World Investment Report* (New York: United Nations, 1991), p. 3.

CHAPTER EIGHT

1. Stewart A. Duncan, *Investment Performance in Canada: Understanding the Big Picture* (Calgary: Canada West Foundation, 1972), p. 2.

2. The Conference Board of Canada forecasts that Canada will experience the lowest economic growth among Group of Seven nations through the end of 1993, with 1.0 percent growth in 1992 and 3.4 percent in 1993. See the *Financial Post*, May 22, 1992, p. 3.

3. The marketing boards affect poultry, eggs, and dairy products. Kentucky Fried Chicken has complained that Canada is the only country in the world where it experiences a major supply problem, and this is due to the marketing boards. Canadian chicken is currently twice as expensive as U.S. chicken. See the *Financial Post*, May 25, 1992, p. 13.

J.D. Forbes, an economist at the University of British Columbia, estimates that British Columbia Milk Board pricing policies provide on average $70,000 (C) in annual subsidies to each B.C. dairy farmer. He has calculated that if import quotas were replaced by tariffs as the General Agreement on Tariffs and Trade has suggested, butter would have a 292 percent tariff, cheddar cheese a 242 percent tariff, imported skim milk a 193 percent tariff, and chicken a 75 percent tariff. A 1990 GATT study estimated that Canadians pay 100 percent above the world price for milk and 20 percent above for eggs. See the *Ottawa Citizen*, May 25, 1992, p. A9.

4. The Maastricht Agreement calls for an inflation rate no more than 1.5 percentage points higher than the average of the three fittest EC countries (Canada would qualify), long-term interest rates no more than 2 percentage points above the average of the three countries with the lowest rates (qualify), a budget deficit below 3 percent of GDP (fail), a government debt below 60 percent of GDP (fail), and a currency that has stayed within the "narrow band" of the European exchange-rate mechanism (fail). See the *Globe and Mail*, May 29, 1992, p. A16.

5. Office of the U.S. Trade Representative, *Foreign Trade Barriers* (Washington, D.C.: Government Printing Office, 1992).

6. *Globe and Mail*, January 24, 1992, p. B2. Without economic growth, some of the benefit derived from lower interest rates is offset by a decline in tax revenues.

7. Banks will now be able to own trust companies, both banks and trusts will be permitted to purchase insurance companies (although selling insurance at local branches will be limited), insurance, trust, and loan companies will acquire full consumer lending powers and expanded commercial lending powers, and banks and trusts will be permitted to sell goods and services, including insurance, to their credit-card holders.

BIBLIOGRAPHY

Abele, Frances, ed. *How Ottawa Spends: The Politics of Competitiveness 1992–93*. Ottawa: Carleton University Press, 1992.

Abele, Frances, ed. *How Ottawa Spends: The Politics of Fragmentation 1991–92*. Ottawa: Carleton University Press, 1991.

Balthazar, Louis, Guy Laforest, and Vincent Lemieux, eds. *Le Québec et la restructuration du Canada 1980–1992: Enjeux et perspectives*. Sillery, Qué.: Septentrion, 1991.

Barlow, Maude and Bruce Campbell. *Take Back the Nation*. Toronto: Key Porter, 1991.

Bélanger, Yves, and Pierre Hamel, eds. *Québec 2000: Quel développement?* Sillery, Qué.: Presses de l'Université du Québec, 1992.

Bélisle, Jean-Pierre. *Savoir pour choisir*. Sainte-Thérèse, Qué.: Serdev, 1992.

Bercuson, David J., and Barry Cooper. *Deconfederation: Canada without Quebec*. Toronto: Key Porter, 1991.

Bissonnette, Lise. *La passion du présent*. Montréal: Boréal Express, 1987.

Brock, Kathy L. "The Politics of Aboriginal Self-Government: A Canadian Paradox." *Canadian Public Administration* 34 (Summer 1991): 272–285.

Brown, Douglas M., ed. *Canada: The State of the Federation 1991*. Kingston, Ont.: Queen's University Institute of Intergovernmental Relations, 1991.

Cairns, Alan C. *Charter versus Federalism: The Dilemmas of Constitutional Reform*. Montreal: McGill-Queen's University Press, 1992.

Cairns, Alan C. *Disruptions: Constitutional Struggles, from the Charter to Meech Lake*. Toronto: McClelland & Stewart, 1991.

Cameron, Norman, E. J. Chambers, Derek Hum, John McCallum, Doug May, M. B. Percy, Dane Rowlands, and Wayne Simpson. *From East and West: Regional Views on Reconfederation*. Toronto: C.D. Howe Institute, 1991.

Cassidy, Frank, ed. *Aboriginal Self-Determination*. Halifax: Oolichan Books and the Institute for Research on Public Policy, 1991.

Charlton, Mark, and Paul Barker, eds. *Contemporary Political Issues*. Scarborough, Ont.: Nelson Canada, 1991.

Citizens' Forum on Canada's Future. *Report to the People and Government of Canada*. Ottawa: Minister of Supply and Services Canada, 1991.

Cloutier, Édouard, Jean H. Guay, and Daniel Latouche. *Le virage: L'évolution de l'opinion publique au Québec depuis 1960*. Montréal: Québec/Amérique, 1992.

Cohen, Andrew. A Deal Undone: *The Making and Breaking of the Meech Lake Accord*. Vancouver: Douglas & McIntyre, 1990.

Coleman, William D. *The Independence Movement in Quebec 1945–1980*. Toronto: University of Toronto Press, 1984.

Constitutional Committee of the Québec Liberal Party. *A Québec Free to Choose*. Report submitted to the twenty-fifth Convention of the Québec Liberal Party, January 1991.

Courtney, John, Peter MacKinnon, and David E. Smith, eds. *After Meech Lake: Lessons for the Future*. Saskatoon, Sask.: Fifth House, 1991.

Doern, Bruce G., and Bryne B. Purchase. *Canada at Risk?* Ottawa: Renouf, 1991.

Doran, Charles F., "Canada's Role in North America." *Current History* (December 1991): 401–404.

Doran, Charles F. and Alvin Paul Drischler, eds. *The United States, Canada, and the World Economy*. Washington, D.C.: SAIS Foreign Policy Institute, 1991.

Dufour, Christian. *A Canadian Challenge, Le défi québécois*. Halifax: Institute for Research on Public Policy, 1990.

Dufresne, Jacques. *Le courage et la lucidité*. Sillery, Qué: Septentrion, 1990.

Dyck, Rand. *Provincial Politics in Canada*. 2d ed. Scarborough, Ont.: Prentice Hall Canada, 1991.

Echenberg, Havi, Arthur Milner, John Myles, Lars Osberg, Shelley Phipps, John Richards, and William B. P. Robson. *A Social Charter for Canada? Perspectives on the Constitutional Entrenchment of Social Rights*. Toronto: C.D. Howe Institute, 1992.

Fidler, Richard. *Canada, Adieu?* Lantzville, British Columbia: Oolichan Books, 1991.

Fournier, Pierre. *A Meech Lake Post-Mortem: Is Quebec Sovereignty Inevitable?* Montreal and Kingston, Ont.: McGill-Queen's University Press, 1991.

Friesen, John W. *The Cultural Maze: Complex Questions on Native Destiny in Western Canada*. Calgary: Detselig Enterprises, 1991.

Frizzell, Alan, Jon H. Pammett, and Anthony Westell. *The Canadian General Election of 1988*. Ottawa: Carleton University Press, 1989.

Fry, Earl H. *The Canadian Political System*. Washington, D.C.: Association for Canadian Studies in the United States, 1991.

Gagnon, Alain-G., and François Rocher, eds. *Répliques aux détracteurs de la souveraineté du Québec*. Montréal: VLB Éditeur, 1992.

Gagnon, Lysiane. *Chroniques politiques*. Montréal: Boréal Express, 1985.

Gairdner, William D. *The Trouble with Canada*. Toronto: General Paperbacks, 1991.

Gibbins, Roger. *Conflict and Unity: An Introduction to Canadian Political Life*. 2d ed. Scarborough, Ont.: Nelson Canada, 1990.

Gibbins, Roger, ed. *Meech Lake and Canada: Perspectives from the West*. Edmonton: Academic Printing and Publishing, 1988.

Granatstein, J. L., Irving M. Abella, T. W. Acheson, David J. Bercuson, R. Craig Brown, and H. Blair Neatby. *Nation: Canada Since Confederation*. 3d ed. Toronto: McGraw-Hill Ryerson, 1990.

Granatstein, J. L., and Norman Hillmer. *For Better or For Worse: Canada and the United States to the 1990s*. Toronto: Copp Clark Pitman, 1991.

Grant, George. *Lament for a Nation: The Defeat of Canadian Nationalism*. Reprint. Toronto: Gage, 1978.

Gregg, Allan, and Michael Posner. *The Big Picture: What Canadians Think about Almost Everything*. Toronto: Macfarlane Walter & Ross, 1990.

Hampson, Fen Osler, and Christopher J. Maule, eds. *Canada among Nations 1992–93: A New World Order?* Ottawa: Carleton University Press, 1992.

Harris, Richard G., and Douglas D. Purvis. "Constitutional Change and Canada's Economic Prospects." *Canadian Public Policy* 17 (December 1991): 379–394.

Hawkes, David C., ed. *Aboriginal Peoples and Government Responsibility*. Ottawa: Carleton University Press, 1991.

Heard, Andrew. *Canadian Constitutional Conventions: The Marriage of Law and Politics*. Toronto: Oxford University Press, 1991.

Hiller, Harry H. *Canadian Society: A Macro Analysis*. 2d ed. Scarborough, Ont.: Prentice Hall Canada, 1991.

Hirche, Todd. *The Economics of Quebec Separation: Consequences for Quebec and the Rest of Canada*. Calgary: Canada West Foundation, 1992.

Horry, Isabella D., and Michael A. Walker. *Government Spending Facts*. Vancouver: Fraser Institute, 1991.

Hufbauer, Gary Clyde, and Jeffrey J. Schott. *North American Free Trade*. Washington, D.C.: Institute for International Economics, 1992.

Hunter, Robert, and Robert Calihoo. *Occupied Canada*. Toronto: McClelland & Stewart, 1991.

Ip, Irene K. *Big Spenders: A Survey of Provincial Government Finances in Canada*. Toronto: C.D. Howe Institute, 1991.

Jockel, Joseph T. "Canada in the Post–Cold War World." *Current History* (December 1991): 405–410.

Jockel, Joseph T. "Canada-U.S. Relations in the Bush Era." *Canadian American Public Policy*. Number 1. Orono: University of Maine Press, April 1990.

Laidler, David E. W., and William B.P. Robson. *Two Nations, One Money?* Toronto: C.D. Howe Institute, 1991.

Lamont, Lansing, and J. Duncan Edmonds. *Friends So Different: Essays on Canada and the United States in the 1980s*. Ottawa: University of Ottawa Press: 1989.

Lemco, Jonathan. "Turmoil in the Peaceable Kingdom: The Quebec Sovereignty Movement and Its Implications for Canada and the United States." *Canada-U.S. Outlook*, nos. 1, 2 (March 1992).

Leslie, Peter. *Federal State, National Economy*. Toronto: University of Toronto Press, 1987.

Levy, Gary, and Graham White, eds. *Provincial and Territorial Legislatures in Canada*. Toronto: University of Toronto Press, 1989.

Lipset, Seymour Martin. *Continental Divide: The Values and Institutions of the United States and Canada*. New York: Routledge, 1990.

Lisée, Jean-François. *In the Eye of the Eagle*. Toronto: HarperCollins, 1990.

Mahler, Gregory S., and Roman R. March, eds. *Canadian Politics 91/92*. Guilford, CT: Dushkin, 1991.

Marmor, Theodore R. "Canada's Health-Care System: A Model for the United States?" *Current History* (December 1991): 422–427.

Mathews, Georges. *L'Accord: Comment Robert Bourassa fera l'indépendance*. Montréal: Le Jour, 1990.

Mathews, Georges. *Quiet Resolution: Québec's Challenge to Canada*. Toronto: Summerhill Press, 1990.

McCallum, John, and Chris Green. *Parting as Friends: The Economic Consequences for Quebec*. Toronto: C.D. Howe Institute, 1991.

McDougall, John N. "North American Integration and Canadian Disunity." *Canadian Public Policy* 17 (December 1991): 395–408.

McKie, Craig, and Keith Thompson, eds. *Canadian Social Trends*. Toronto: Thompson Educational, 1990.

McRoberts, Kenneth. "Canada's Constitutional Crisis." *Current History* (December 1991): 411–416.

McRoberts, Kenneth. *Quebec: Social Change and Political Crisis*. 3d ed. Toronto: McClelland & Stewart, 1988.

Milne, David. *Tug of War: Ottawa and the Provinces under Trudeau and Mulroney.* Toronto: James Lorimer, 1986.

Monahan, Patrick J. *Meech Lake: The Inside Story.* Toronto: University of Toronto Press, 1991.

Monière, Denis. *L'indépendance.* Montréal: Québec/Amérique, 1992.

Morici, Peter. "Managing the Transition to Free Trade." *Current History* (December 1991): 428–431.

Morici, Peter. *A New Special Relationship: Free Trade and U.S.-Canada Economic Relations in the 1990s.* Ottawa: Carleton University Centre for Trade Policy and Law, 1991.

Morrison, Alex, ed. *Divided We Fall: The National Security Implications of Canadian Constitutional Issues.* Toronto: Canadian Institute of Strategic Studies, 1992.

Oliver, Michael. *The Passionate Debate: The Social and Political Ideas of Quebec Nationalism, 1920–1945.* Montreal: Véhicule Press, 1991.

Ouellet, Fernand. *Economy, Class, & Nation in Quebec: Interpretive Essays.* Toronto: Copp Clark Pitman, 1991.

Québec Ministère des Affaires internationales. *La libéralisation des échanges commerciaux entre le Canada, les États-Unis, et le Mexique: Les enjeux dans une perspective québécoise.* Québec: Ministère des Affaires internationales, 1992.

Québec Ministère du Commerce extérieur et du Développement technologique. *The Canada-United States Free Trade Agreement: A Québec Viewpoint.* Québec: Commerce extérieur et Développement technologique, 1988.

Radwanski, George and Julia Luttrell. *The Will of a Nation.* Toronto: Stoddart, 1992.

Richards, John, François Vaillancourt, and William G. Watson. *Survival: Official Language Rights in Canada.* Toronto: C.D. Howe Institute, 1992.

Ritchie, Gordon, Ronald J. Wonnacott, W. H. Furtan, R. S. Gray, Richard G. Lipsey, and Rodrigue Tremblay. *Broken Links: Trade Relations after a Quebec Secession.* Toronto: C.D. Howe Institute, 1991.

Rosenblum, Simon, and Peter Findlay, eds. *Debating Canada's Future: Views from the Left.* Toronto: Lorimer, 1991.

Russell, Peter H. "Can the Canadians Be a Sovereign People?" *Canadian Journal of Political Science* 24 (December 1991): 691–709.

Russell, Peter H., Rainer Knopff, and Ted Morton. *Federalism and the Charter.* Ottawa: Carleton University Press, 1990.

Savoie, Donald J. *The Politics of Public Spending in Canada.* Toronto: University of Toronto Press, 1990.

Schwartz, Mildred A. "Canadian Society: Trouble in Paradise." *Current History* (December 1991): 417–421.

Scowen, Reed. *A Different Vision: The English in Quebec in the 1990s*. Don Mills, Ont.: Maxwell Macmillan Canada, 1991.

Simeon, Richard, and Mary Janigan, eds. *Toolkits and Building Blocks: Constructing a New Canada*. Toronto: C.D. Howe Institute, 1991.

Smiley, D. V. *The Federal Condition in Canada*. Toronto: McGraw-Hill Ryerson, 1987.

Smith, David E., Peter MacKinnon, and John C. Courtney, eds. *After Meech Lake: Lessons for the Future*. Saskatoon, Sask.: Fifth House, 1991.

Sokolsky, Joel J. "Ogdensburg plus Fifty and Still Counting: Canada-U.S. Defense Relations in the Post–Cold War Era." *Canadian American Public Policy*. Number 8. Orono: University of Maine Press, December 1991.

Special Joint Committee of the Senate and the House of Commons. *A Renewed Canada*. Ottawa: Supply and Services Canada, February 1992.

Stevenson, Garth. *Unfulfilled Union: Canadian Federalism and National Unity*. 3d ed. Toronto: Gage Educational, 1989.

Valaskakis, Kimon. *Canada in the Nineties: Meltdown or Renaissance?* Montreal: Gamma Institute Press, 1990.

Watts, Ronald L., and Douglas M. Brown, eds. *Canada: The State of the Federation 1990*. Kingston, Ont.: Queen's University Institute of Intergovernmental Relations, 1990.

Watts, Ronald L., and Douglas M. Brown, eds. *Options for a New Canada*. Toronto: University of Toronto Press, 1991.

Weaver, R. Kent, Keith G. Banting, Stéphane Dion, and Andrew Stark. *The Collapse of Canada?* Washington D.C.: Brookings Institution, 1992.

Whalley, John. "Now that the Deal Is Over: Canadian Trade Policy Options in the 1990s." *Canadian Public Policy* 16 (June 1990): 121–136.

White, Randall. *Voice of Region: The Long Journey to Senate Reform in Canada*. Toronto: Dundurn Press, 1990.

INDEX

Campeau, Jean, 36
Canada, 49, 51, 53; economic conditions, 10, 11, 12–13, 15–16, 52–53, 64, 68; economic policies, 9, 22, 51–52, 65; foreign opinion of, 2, 16, 63, 69; government, 59–60; society, 45, 56, 58; trade with, 4, 65, 68
Canada Clause, 24
"Canada's Future Together," 22
Canadian Manufacturers' Association, 43–44
Canadian opinion, 56, 62; of government, 11, 51, 58, 59–60; of Quebec, 16, 20–21, 23, 32, 38; of United States, 13, 22, 60, 63–64
Capital flight, 11
Central Canada, 49–51, 53
Charter of Rights and Freedoms, 17, 18, 19, 37
Charter of the French Language (Bill 101), 20, 31–32
Chrétien, Jean, 58
Citizen's Forum on Canada's Future, 22, 59–60
Citizenship, 28
Civil rights, 20, 37, 40
Clark, Joe, 23, 26
Commission de protection de la langue francaise, 31
Communism: fear of, 3
Competitiveness: Canadian, 12, 41, 43, 45–47, 53, 70
Conseil du Patronat, 57
Conservative party. See Progressive Conservative party
Constitution (Canada): proposed changes to, 1–2, 18, 20–25, 44, 68, 69
Constitution Act (1867), 18, 19, 45

Constitution Act (1982), 18–19, 20
Construction industry, 44
Consumers, 9, 10, 44
Corporations (American), 17, 69; in Canada, 10, 11, 41, 52, 61, 62
Corporations (Canadian), 36, 46; foreign ownership of, 5, 61, 62; in United States, 5–6
Council of the Federation, 22
Courts of appeal, 18, 32
Credit unions, 29
Cree Indians, 33–34
Cuomo, Mario, 34
Dairy industry, 35
Debt, 43. See also Public debt
Defense budget, 42
Desjardins credit union movement, 29
Devolution of powers, 1, 10, 19, 20, 22, 24–25, 45, 68
Diefenbaker, John, 2
Dion, Léon, 27
Distinct society clause, 19, 20, 22, 24, 28, 58
Dobbie-Beaudoin Committee, 22–23
Dropouts from school, 35, 54, 57–59
Durham, John George Lambton, Earl, 28

Economic Council of Canada, 45, 57
Economic development, 25, 29, 47, 67
Economic nationalism, 62–64
Economic power, 29, 44, 51–52
Economic union, 10, 44–45, 69–70
Edmonton (Alt.), 56
Education, 29, 31, 32, 33, 35–36, 54, 57–58, 63
Eisenhower, Dwight, 2
Elections, 16–17, 19, 52. See also Referendum
Elizabeth II, queen of Great Britain, 19

GROUP of SEVEN: Canada, France, Germany, Japan, Italy, U.K., U.S.
(Bilateral)
FTA = US/Canada Free Trade Agreement
NAFTA = US/Can/Mexico
PPP = purchasing power parity - what the average paycheck will buy in terms of a basket of goods and services -
Ranks: 1) US 2) Canada

27.5 million Canadians